Student's Classroom Handbook For The Kingdoms & The Elves Of The Reaches

Robert Stanek

Keeper Martin's Tales

This is a work of fiction. All the characters, names, places and events portrayed in this book are either products of the author's imagination or are used fictitiously. Any resemblance to any actual locale, person or event is entirely coincidental.

**Student's Classroom Handbook For
The Kingdoms & The Elves Of The Reaches
(Keeper Martin's Tales, Book 1)**

Copyright © 2003 by Robert Stanek

First Edition, October 2003

All rights reserved, including the right to reproduce this book, or portions thereof, in any form. Printed in the United States of America.

Ruin Mist Publications
Published by Virtual Press, Inc.

Cover design & illustration by Robert Stanek
ISBN 1-57545-033-X

Ruin Mist Publications grants classroom teachers the right to reproduce copies of materials from Word Search, Word Sort, Word Jumble, Words to Watch For (vocab list) and Review Questions for Discussion sections of this book for classroom use only. No other part of this publication may be reproduced in whole or in part.

The reproduction of any part for an entire school or school system is strictly prohibited. No part of this publication may be transmitted, stored, or recorded in any form without written permission from the publisher.

Young Adult Books by Robert Stanek

Keeper Martin's Tales
The Kingdoms & the Elves of the Reaches
The Kingdoms & the Elves of the Reaches II
The Kingdoms & the Elves of the Reaches III
The Kingdoms & the Elves of the Reaches IV

Ruin Mist Tales
The Elf Queen & the King I
The Elf Queen & the King II

Magic Lands: Journey Beyond the Beyond
Ruin Mist Heroes, Legends & Beyond
Magic Lands & Other Stories

Praise for Ruin Mist

"A gem waiting to be unearthed by millions of fans of fantasy!"

"Brilliant... an absolutely superior tale of fantasy for all tastes!"

"It's a creative, provoking, and above all, thoughtful story!"

"It's a wonderful metaphor for the dark (and light) odyssey of the mind."

"The fantasy world you have created is truly wonderful and rich. Your characters seem real and full of life."

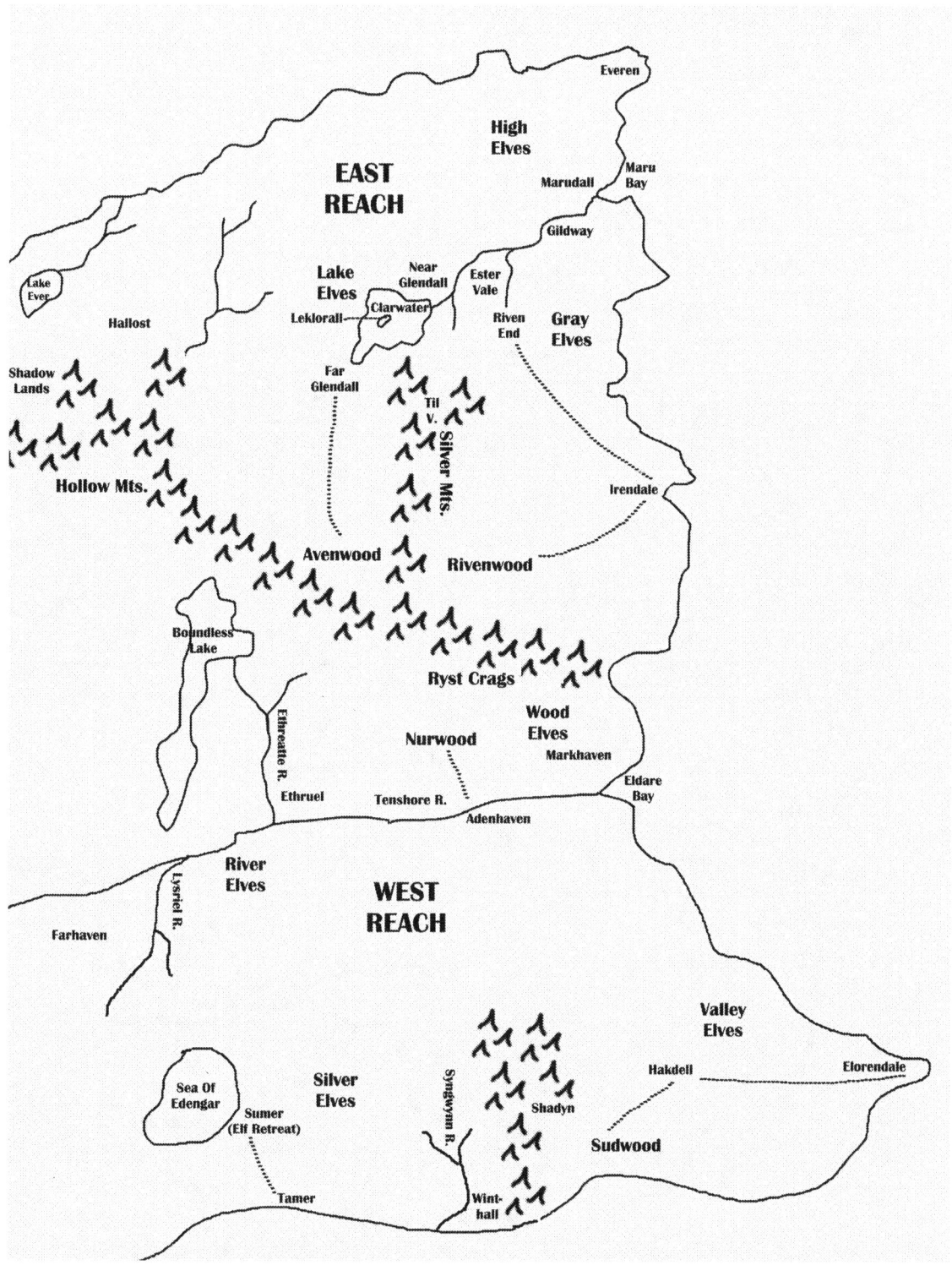

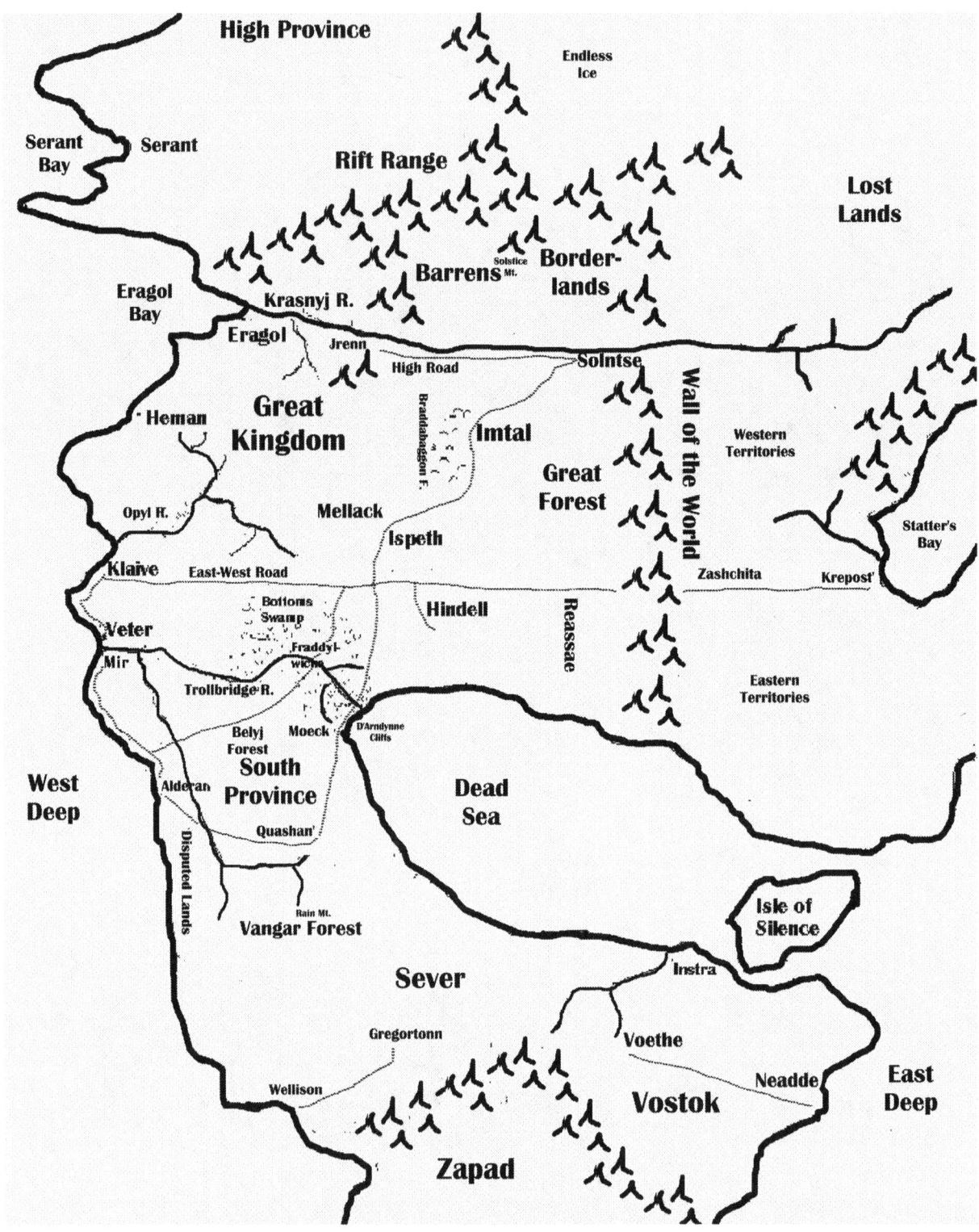

Table Of Contents

INTRODUCTION 9

CHAPTER ONE: THOSE DESTINED 10

CHAPTER TWO: THE WINDS OF CHANGE 18

CHAPTER THREE: IT BEGINS 27

CHAPTER FOUR: DISCOVERY 38

CHAPTER FIVE: REALIZATION 45

CHAPTER SIX: PERMISSION 55

CHAPTER SEVEN: MEETING 62

CHAPTER EIGHT: GUIDANCE 68

CHAPTER NINE: AMBUSH 77

CHAPTER TEN: FIRST LESSONS 82

CHAPTER ELEVEN: DECISION 91

CHAPTER TWELVE: VANGAR FOREST 99

CHAPTER THIRTEEN: THE BOTTOMS 105

CHAPTER FOURTEEN: REST'S END 110

CHAPTER FIFTEEN: DISASTER 115

CHAPTER SIXTEEN: RETURN 120

Meet Robert Stanek

Robert Stanek was born in Burlington, Wisconsin. His father was an entrepreneur who immigrated to America from Budapest, Hungary. His mother is the granddaughter of French and Norwegian immigrants. He attended various schools, and joined the United States Air Force at the age of 19. He served in the Persian Gulf War, and earned many medals for his wartime service, including the highest-flying honor, the Air Force Distinguished Flying Cross. After the war, he attended university, earning his bachelor's and master's degrees in only 3 years.

As a boy, he dreamed of being a writer. In elementary school, he was a junior editor for the school newspaper. Although he has written many books for professionals since 1994, his works of fiction have quickly become his most popular books. His first novel was *Keeper Martin's Tale*, which was simultaneously released in adult and children's editions. He describes the book as "a story of mystery, intrigue, magic, and adventure." Many of his other works of fiction are also fantasies, set in incredibly fantastic worlds.

Introduction

Welcome to the *Student's Classroom Handbook for The Kingdoms & the Elves of the Reaches*! If you are holding this book in your hands, you are in for a most amazing adventure so get ready for fantastic journeys, strange happenings and edge-of-your seat views into the fantastic world of Ruin Mist.

As you prepare to meet wonderful new friends, like Adrina, Vilmos, Seth, Galan and Emel, keep in mind that this student guide is designed to help you have fun and learn. Inside this book, you'll find the complete text of *The Kingdoms & the Elves of the Reaches (Keeper Martin's Tale, Book 1)*. After each chapter, you'll find fun activities that help you build vocabulary and learn new skills.

After reading this book, you may want to go on to read *The Kingdoms & the Elves of the Reaches II*, *The Kingdoms & the Elves of the Reaches III* and *The Kingdoms & the Elves of the Reaches IV*. In fact, we hope you will, so don't miss out on the opportunity at the end of this book to win free copies of the other books for your school. Just for entering, you could win a cool Ruin Mist T-Shirt, Hat or Poster from the Ruin Mist Gear shop (http://www.cafeshops.com/ruinmistgear).

Thank you, and have fun!

Words to Watch

Feral	Trustworthy	Dominate
Edifice	Surreptitiously	Levitate
Portcullis	Feat	Solitude
Fleeting	Warden	Indignity
Ransom	Century	
Incursion	Ancestral	

Chapter One: Those Destined

Sunrise loomed across the horizon, pale as jasmine and mostly obscured by dark, feral clouds. The early morning air held an unusual chill and Adrina gathered her light shawl more closely as she stepped out onto the catwalk atop the wall. A stout breeze blew long strands of hair across her face. The hair, black as the receding night, flowed to her waist and while it was normally braided and folded over her left shoulder, it wasn't now.

Summer must surely be at an end, Adrina surmised, for the breeze came from the North and not from the West Deep.

Adrina walked to a place where the wall jutted out and cut its way into High King's Square. Behind her the palace parade grounds were empty and silent, as was the square before her. The silence seemed a shroud over the whole of Imtal clear to the Braddabaggon foothills. Many stories below, the city's residents would soon awake. The square would fill with sounds as merchants began to unpack their wares. Palace guardsmen would muster for breakfast. City and palace would stir to life.

Yet Adrina preferred the empty moments just before all this happened, for the silence echoed the aching of her heart. She pressed her chin into the palm of her hand, her elbow glued to the stone framework of the wall. She sighed mournfully. The palace was truly dead, all *real* life having long since been gnawed away.

She could have passed the day dreaming about things beyond the gray stone edifice, the cold palace wall, with its portcullis tucked cleanly out of view. She had sauntered through many a day thus, envisioning magnificent journeys to the four corners of the land.

Great Kingdom had many holdings. High Province in the North—the far, far North—where amidst mountains of ice and stone the rivers boiled and filled the air with blankets of fog. South, beyond a forest of great white trees called giant birch, lay South Province with its capital city enveloped by the majestic Quashan' valley. East through the Kingdom along the East-West road were the Territories, divided east and west. The untamed Eastern Territories were awaiting discovery. The Western Territories held but two Kingdom outposts: Zashchita and Krepost'. Traders claimed the walled city of Zashchita was carved from the very trees of the forest and its building lifted so far into the heavens that they were lost in the clouds. Beyond Zashchita lay Krepost' and her ferryman who took travelers across River Krepost' so they could begin the climb into the mountain city, and where afterward the gatekeeper may or may not chase them over the cliffs into Statter's Bay and to their deaths.

But today Adrina was frustrated to the point of tears. She wouldn't pass the day dreaming of things she may never see. She didn't understand what difference the passing of a year made. Why did it matter so that she was a year older? This year seemed the same as the last.

She would have done anything, given anything, to be a little girl again, free to wander the city in her brother's shadow. Together they would wander Imtal's cobbled streets. She would pretend not to notice the press of guardsmen around them and see only those who had come out to greet them.

A fleeting smile lit her face. She knew this could be no more. Valam was gone now, gone to South Province, gone for good, and she, Adrina, was leaving adolescence.

The echo of footsteps against hard stones startled her. Her eyes went wide and she wondered if Lady Isador would venture to the walls. Her governess had threatened to before.

Adrina didn't want to be reminded of all the things she should or should not do, so she slipped away to the northern watchtower. At dawn the tower would be vacant and she could be alone without fear of interruption.

Adrina wound her way up a long spiral staircase. She stopped only at the very top to catch her breath. Here at the landing was a large, open chamber whose broad windows were normally used to keep watch on the city's north wall and the fields beyond. Adrina crossed the empty chamber to a window. The cool breeze on her face tingled her nose and brushed the sweat away.

"No lessons today," she whispered to the wind. Lessons Chancellor Yi and Lady Isador would surely chastise her for missing them—if they found her.

Not today, Adrina vowed, not today.

Always more reminders of the things she should or should not do—her proper place, always her proper place. She knew all about the proper things, the proper mannerisms, the proper greetings, her proper duties, her proper place. She had even been taught, though only recently, the proper things to do to invite a man's attention. She was to begin courting. But why?

What did she need a man for? Moreover, what would she do with one once she caught him? Was there anything she couldn't do on her own?

Leave Imtal, the wind seemed to say. That was right; on her own, she would never leave Imtal. The palace would be all she would see for the rest of her days, but did it have to be this way?

The wind howling in answer spurred Adrina on. "Courtship, marriage," she shouted back, "maybe it wouldn't be so bad, for surely all suitors don't live in Imtal."

As quickly as she said it, Adrina cast the notion away. Marriage had taken Calyin away. Adrina told the wind, "No, that's not for me."

She reveled in memories now, slipping back into the past and a time when everything seemed simpler. The minutes slipped away, and then Adrina pictured a beautiful sad face. Tears came to her eyes. Simpler times were not easier times.

"Why mother, why did you have to go? I have never forgiven you, never, and I never will. I am all alone now. Calyin is wed. Valam is in the South. Midori went away, never to return. And you, you are… gone. What am I to do? Can you know how much I loved you? And you always in that stupid garden."

Adrina waited. The wind howled, but no answer came.

"Queen Alexandria was beautiful. Land and people loved her very dear," said a figure from the shadows.

Adrina screamed; her heart stopped. Then in a sudden flood of thoughts, her young mind began to race—surely this must be a rogue come to steal her away.

Adrina said coyly, and hoped the other knew she wasn't telling the truth, "What manner of rogue are you? My father would hardly pay ransom for his third daughter. I am of little worth."

The robed figure still enveloped in shadows spoke again. "By the Mother, I never heard such a thing."

The figure moved toward Adrina who edged closer and closer to the open window behind her.

"Child, I will not harm you."

"Who are you and what are you doing here?" Adrina asked, brushing back hair from her eyes. "Your face it is covered in soot. Stop where you are or I will scream again."

"Go ahead, none will hear. I come to speak to you, Highness. I have seen you standing in this tower often."

"Who are you?"

"I live here. I clean. You *will* journey beyond Imtal. I have seen you in a far off place."

"Seen me?"

"In a dream… Smell the wind."

"Smell, the wind?"

"Child, smell it. It comes, can you not tell?"

"It?"

The strange woman took Adrina's hand and turned her to the window. The chill breeze was still howling out of the North. "Change, child. Sadness cannot hold forever the land."

Adrina turned to look at the woman's face. The woman directed Adrina's gaze away and pointed to the distant horizon. Adrina stared long. She imagined she could see Solstice Mountain and the whole of the Rift Range. In her dreams, she had journeyed there. The border country all around Great Kingdom was wild, to the north especially so. The sole purpose of the elite High Road Garrison Guardsmen was to provide travelers with safe passage along the Kingdom's High Road and to shield the Kingdom from bandit incursions out of the north. Beyond High Road was a vast desert called the Barrens, a no man's land. Beyond the Barrens was the untiring Rift Range—ice-capped mountains of jagged black rock that climbed perilously into the heavens. Or so she had been told.

"Is that where I'll journey to?" Adrina asked, turning around. The woman was gone. "Hello?… Are you still here?"

The chill north wind howled. Adrina turned eyes filled with expectations back to the fields beyond Imtal. Calyin had told her once that in the North there were mountains that breathed rivers of fire.

Hearing what sounded like a foot slipping across the stones of the floor, Adrina spun around. "Hello? Hello?" she called out.

From the shadows the woman whispered, "Be careful what you wish for."

Adrina stepped toward the woman. "What do you mean?"

The woman, her face suddenly appearing aged beyond her years, took Adrina's hand. She kneeled then and as she kissed Adrina's hand, Adrina felt the moisture of tears on her arm. The woman whispered, "I cry for the children who at the end of the journey will never be the same. Child, I cry for you. I cry because I see you standing in the midst of a killing field. I cry for the thousands dead at your feet…"

***

Crying out into the darkness, alone, afraid and drenched in sweat, Vilmos awoke. His thoughts raced. The whole of his small body shivered uncontrollably. Opening eyes and uncurling his huddled form from a corner, moist with his own perspiration yet still cold from the night's chill, was a slow, time-consuming process.

"It was only a nightmare," Vilmos whispered to reassure himself—a nightmare like no other. In the dream he had used the forbidden magic once too often and the Priests of the Dark Flame—opposers of all that is magic and magical—came from their temples to slay him.

Vilmos stood uneasily and dipped trembling hands into the washbasin beside the bed. The cool water sucked the hurt from his eyes and mind and gently began to soothe and awaken his senses as nothing else could.

Carefully he dabbed a wet cloth to the corners of his eyes and only then did he became something other than the frightened boy who in his dreams huddled into the forlorn corner because of the sense of security it gave him to know his back was against the wall and that nothing could sneak up on him from behind.

Only then that he became the boy of twelve whose name was Vilmos. Vilmos because it was a trustworthy name. Vilmos because it was his father's name, who was named Vilmos because it had been his father's name. Vilmos, the Counselor's son.

Readying for the day's chores, Vilmos pushed the last of the dream from his thoughts. He dressed quickly and slipped on his ill-fitting boots as he stumbled toward the kitchen.

The aroma of fresh-baked black bread and honey cakes pungent in the air about the kitchen, mixing with the growling of his stomach, made him aware of an enormous hunger. The night had been unbearably long and he had not eaten since supper of the previous day.

"Late again. You'll sleep your life away. Already an hour past first light," said his mother. She stood in front of the hearth. The words were not meant to be harsh, nor were they taken thus. They were a standard greeting.

"I know mother, I am sorry," replied Vilmos, tossing gnarled hair to one side surreptitiously, hair that should have been combed. He started to hurry away.

"Vilmos, where are you going?" Lillath asked. "Must I always remind you of your lessons? Someday you will fill your father's position. Someday you will be Counselor of Tabborrath Village. Now, recite the lore of the peoples."

"Mother, do I have to?"

Lillath didn't say anything, she just stared.

"Can I use the book?"

"From memory."

"The tale of the four peoples is the lore of four kingdoms," Vilmos began, beaming with Lillath's smile upon him. "Small in number, strong of will, united they stood against powerful kingdoms of the North. Four vast kingdoms would conquer the four peoples, but the will of the four peoples was too strong. Lycya, mightiest of the kingdoms, was swallowed by barren desert. North Reach and the clans over-mountain were consumed by the twenty-year snow. Queen of Elves and all her people were washed into West Deep by the three-year rain. Only the Alder's kingdom, once the smallest kingdom of the North, survives.

"To survive, the Alder's kingdom formed an alliance with the four peoples. Their Graces, King Alexas of Yug, King Jarom of Vostok, King Peter of Zapad and his Royal Majesty, King Charles of Sever, are the wardens of the four peoples. The four wardens maintain the alliance and protect the four peoples."

Lillath maintained her smile. "Well, yes," she said, "that is the lore of the four kingdoms and thus the tale of four peoples. But it is not *the* lore of the Four Peoples. You need to take great care in your listening. Listening is the counselor's greatest skill. Each tale, each bit of lore, tells a lesson. Relate the lesson through the lore; it is the way of the counselor. Choose the wrong tale, give the wrong advice. Do you understand?"

"Yes, mother."

"Now tell me the correct tale and guess the lesson."

Nervously Vilmos played his tongue against his cheek. "From memory?"

"You may use the book if need be, at times even your father reads from the book."

"Mother," began Vilmos, looking into her eyes with much sincerity, "is it not time to—"

"Run along," she said. "Wood for the day's fire." There was a hint of mirth in her voice as she watched him wet his hands and settle his unruly hair.

Vilmos briefly, but closely, studied his mother's features as he did each morning. Offset by a touch of gray, dark black hair the color of a starless night sky fell to her waist. Her face, ripened with age in a pleasant way, was deep-set with eyes of hazel that seemed always to be calling out. This morning they said, *Hurry along or you'll be late.*

He looked like her not like father, thought Vilmos each morning as he did this—a father who barely tolerated him. Harsh words chased through the boy's mind. "Vilmos, why did you do that? I told you not to!" or "Vilmos, go to your room." With an occasional, "I should send him away," thrown in when his father thought Vilmos couldn't hear.

"He is only a boy," Vilmos often heard in rebuke. "He will change in time. Give him more time." There was a deep love between the two, mother and son.

Wood for the hearth could be gathered easily from the brambles on the edge of the thick woods near the outskirts of the village and it was to this place that Vilmos started to go, but the outside air this morning was chillier than usual and it sent a shiver racing down Vilmos' back. It carried with it sadness and a sudden flood of remembrance. In the back of his mind, Vilmos knew the real reason he watched his mother so closely. One day he would indeed be sent away, far away, because one day the dark priests would come for him.

Vilmos returned to the house to collect his short cloak. As he ran through the kitchen he stopped beside his mother. Rising up on the tips of his toes, he gave her a single peck on her cheek. For an instant, a smile broke her tired face and fondly she touched hand to cheek.

"That's better," Vilmos shouted to no one in particular as he ran outside, slipping the sleeves of his shielding cloak into place. He could endure the cold now, and in a way, the memory as well.

"Hurry, breakfast!" shouted Lillath after him, while unconsciously raising a hand to her cheek once more where soft, young lips had touched. Vilmos looked back only for a moment to see this and to catch her eye. She added as he dashed away, "Remember to be careful… Remember what happened to the girl from Olex Village."

***

Guardedly Seth walked beside Queen Mother. His mind carefully searched while his eyes scanned every shadow the two passed. As First of the Red, her safety was his responsibility. He was against remaining in Sanctuary, but Queen Mother wouldn't speak of leaving.

For reasons that escaped Seth, she wanted to use Sanctuary's High Hall. Its crystalline walls were specially attuned to reflect the feelings of a particular host despite even the best efforts of a mental block or mind shield, and although that was a feat Queen Mother could have easily performed herself, she had said that she wished to conserve her will power. For what, she hadn't said.

Queen Mother, is it true, has he truly returned? Has

Sathar survived the Dark Journey? Seth sent into her mind as he walked.

Even now he joins forces with King Mark of West Reach and still others flock to his banner. It is as we most feared. The time has come… May Father and Mother watch over us…

Will there be war?

Queen Mother regarded Seth. *I will miss you in my thoughts.*

The words caught Seth by surprise. He didn't understand. The link between protector and queen was unbreakable. He was the watch warden of her body and of her mind. He felt her pain. He knew her anguish, her every anxiety. This was *the* link. *My Queen, I don't understand. If you break the link, how will I know if you come to harm? I must be able to find you at all times, no matter the circumstance.*

In time, you will Brother Seth. Even traditions that stem from ages past cannot remain forever. Soon it will be time to guard my own thoughts and my own being, just as the first queen had to do. Centuries ago we abandoned our ancestral homes. We fled to this barren land out of fear. We have lived in fear of repeating the past and only succeeded in repeating it.

Seth was confused and the emotions he cast along with his words showed it. *But my queen, you mustn't. You must direct your will to protect land and people.*

Shh, say no more. We are at High Hall.

The two passed through the outer antechamber and entered High Hall. Seth remained at Queen Mother's side. He was pleased to see Brother Ry'al seated behind Brother Samyuehl, First of the Blue Order.

Greetings, sent Seth to Ry'al, guiding the thought solely to Ry'al's mind. Seth had not seen Ry'al since the two had been together under Samyuehl's tutelage, a time during which Seth had learned a great deal—being of the Red Order meant that he had endured the seven teachings as a member of each order and the training with the Blue had been especially interesting.

Just as Queen Mother took her place and sent her own greetings to the foremost six, each dressed in the appropriately colored robes of their order—Yellow, Brown, Blue, Black, White and Gray—Seth contemplated his long period of tutelage. He then turned to the long rows of cushioned pews to the left and right of the colorful six where the members of High Council sat. As all seemed to be in order, he took his place two paces behind Queen Mother.

High Hall's crystalline walls attuned to Queen Mother's mood. The color spraying forth from the spot where the queen stood, covering the floor, walls and ceiling in a thousand shades of black and gray. When she was certain she had everyone's attention, Queen Mother reached out her hand to the white satin-pillowed couch that dominated the center of the hall. The touch of her hand seemed to melt away the color and then as she levitated in the air above the couch, the white of the satin faded to gray.

For a few moments before he settled behind the shields in his mind, Seth knew and felt Queen Mother's every thought and emotion. She was reminding herself that she had been annoyed this morning and had been annoyed many times over many previous days, but not now. Now she needed to keep her mind clear and her thoughts focused. She needed to keep her emotions centered and directed.

She chose her words carefully now and directed her thoughts outward. *Greetings to wise council. Thank you for a speedy assembly…*

Those words were the last Seth heard before he entered the quiet solitude of his mind. His duty was to be present and not to listen in unless directed to. He had many other things to concern himself with besides squabbles amongst High

Council or the First Brothers. Again, he feared for Queen Mother's safety and wondered what would come of his fears.

Within the folds of his mind, Seth was barely aware of the outside world. Time passed slowly. Then for a single instant, it was as if a breeze had entered his mind—a presence in his thoughts.

Seth opened his eyes and turned to Queen Mother. She regarded him for a moment then dismissed him by saying, *Go now, return to your studies.*

Seth stood his ground, the indignity he felt at the dismissal showing briefly on his face. Then he exited High Hall, speaking not a word.

A time will come when you will know there are things greater than the self, Queen Mother whispered after him, *things greater than our people, and then you will come to terms with the sacrifice I make, but for now return to your studies. You study the ways of Man for a reason. A time of great change comes, a time of change for all. The battle for East Reach is far off, but the battle to save all is already beginning...* She paused momentarily then added, *Call Brother Galan to my chambers.*

Chapter 1: Word Search

Can you find these words in the puzzle?

Incursion	Ancestral	Adrina	Vilmos
Ransom	Century	Imtal	Night
Queen Mother	East Reach	Xith	Princess
Portcullis	Feat	Solitude	Seth
Ebony Lightning	Guards	Keeper Martin	Fun
Prince	Magic	Adventures	King
Edifice	Surreptitiously	Levitate	Emel
Feral	Trustworthy	Dominate	Great Kingdom
Fleeting	Warden	Indignity	Galan
Random	Eleven	Elves	Hands

```
A F F X G A O I S D G H B V C W U M D E A R R Q S F
D R E E M S W B U K L E A I D C V O P D M T S E W T
R J P A R T O N E V B T E L N H W S R I F B X N I R
I M J Y R A Q W D T U N K M L O P I S F A D R V Y U
N T H J U E L R F H G R A O V C N B H I M T A L S S
A H K U Z V F D W R H J N S C A O D E C G P S W C T
D W E T S I L L U C T R O P X Z C Q F E H Y U P L W
R W R L A A E S V M E N F I S H M E L V E S R U N O
F J I E X C E J S T R E E X C Z O Y U G B I M H G R
H U T W S E T H D K E X Y T J L S P U N S N B I G T
K T C I Q P I N H A N D S H A K N G I R R D E A B H
I O L N A V N E L E V E N J W E A N T F D I S S L Y
F L E D D U G A L A N C Y E K L R A M H R G N X Z R
Q U M Q U E E N M O T H E R T W I O B V X N F S A G
T A E Q F R T Y I N C U R S I O N M P I I I U C D T
B E A S T R E A C H H Y R W S A X Z G J T T N V V Y
X C K G N I N T H G I L Y N O B E D R W H Y S D E U
S K L I M O D G N I K T A E R G H U A R C N M O N A
S G T Y I K P C D H J E W G C B R R Z C H Q U M T I
E H K L C E N T U R Y I G U O S D R X I C Z N I U U
C K E E P E R M A R T I N A M E T U I G A L A N R L
N F Y U K V C D P O J L A R N I G H T A S F R A E M
I E D U T I L O S J E X R D B J K E S M A T U T S F
R A N D O M T H O U H G D S E R B N S A I E V E W S
P R I N C E G T A N C E S T R A L E W G N I K L O E
```

Words to Watch

Conscious	Governess	Somber
Chamber	Justification	Cognizant
Principal (Adj.)	Obvious	Imaginary
Habitual	Sympathize	Unfulfilled
Dreary	Contemplate	Conjure
Tradition	Courtier	Sanctuary
Abandon	Aloof	Announcement
Independent	Persistent	Insatiable
Maternal	Meditation	Acknowledgement

Chapter Two: The Winds of Change

Evening found Adrina in the East wing of the palace. She had been wandering its quiet halls for the last few hours. Hunger had roused her to conscious concerns. She still hadn't changed into a dinner gown and the evening meal was less than an hour away. She would have to hurry to meet it, and this she did with urgency. She didn't want to be late, especially after avoiding her duties all day.

Her chambers were on the upper level of the West wing and while Adrina could have gone down two flights of stairs to the ground level and crossed the gardens to the West wing, she decided to use the private royal access ways. Although this route was longer because she had to go through the North wing, she wouldn't have to go up or down any stairs. And she didn't want to stumble into Lady Isador before she changed into her gown—she didn't want to stumble into Lady Isador at all, especially after avoiding her duties all day.

Adrina ran full stride down dark corridors that she knew so well she could have closed her eyes and ran along. There was no fear of bumping into anyone, no one but her used them now, and she knew well ahead of time their every turn by the count of her strides. She turned a sharp corner and knew she was entering the North wing. A mostly straight stretch of hallway was ahead and then another sharp turn—the West wing.

She slowed her gait to catch her breath; the line of light ahead was from the door to her chambers. She stopped outside the door and peeked in. Inside, attendants were waiting to help her with her gown but she didn't see or hear Lady Isador. She paused a moment more to ensure the governess wasn't waiting somewhere out of eyesight, then entered.

The attendants fussed over her hair for a time and helped her put on the gown, but Adrina knew she couldn't wait for them to finish properly. She rushed out of her room even just as they fully secured the ties of the gown around her waist and neck.

She raced so fast down the broad central staircase that she nearly ran down the captain of the guard. She stumbled through a curtsy, and then rushed away.

In the great hall, Andrew, her father, was seated on his kingly chair with its high raised back and stout, straight arms in the true fashion of his office. Catching the gleam in his eye as he looked upon her, Adrina sighed then sat. An attendant pushed her seat forward, and she nodded in response. She was not late, though only barely so.

"Good evening, father," Adrina said, while trying to hide the sudden smile that came to her lips. "I trust I am not late?"

King Andrew swept his gaze around the enormous oblong table to the faces of the honored guests. "Only so, dear Adrina. Only so."

Adrina looked to the stone figurehead that was Chancellor Yi. He stood rigidly behind her father in his rightful place as the king's principal adviser. The old chancellor did not move as he stood there, nor did he ever unless summoned. This was a strange thing since otherwise he was plagued with a habitual cold. A cold complete with runny nose, continuous sniffles and sneezing. A cold that he could turn off and on at will. To Adrina it was a warning sign of the deadening effect of the dreary, gray castle upon the senses, numbing everything away, leaving only the dead and the dying.

She would watch him while she ate, as she often did, searching for that small, scarcely perceivable shift of muscle or limb that told her he was still alive and not quite dead like some of the courtiers who dined with them and might just as well have been made of the cold stones of the gray wall behind her—they cared just about as much.

Her stomach rumbled. Adrina looked to the attendants waiting to ferry food to the tables, knowing that the prayer would come first and waiting for Father Tenuus to rise to his feet and clear his throat.

Father Tenuus was the only member of the priesthood that lived in the palace. Others of the priesthood, like Father Jacob, first priest of Great-Father, had chambers tucked away in the East wing of the palace this was true, but mild times mandated a breaking with old traditions. Now only Father Tenuus remained. The others had long ago abandoned Imtal Palace.

When the aged priest, given to habitual forgetfulness nearly to the point of annoyance, finally began the invocation, Adrina said her own silent prayer. She hoped he'd finish in record time. Her stomach rumbled again. She was hungry, very hungry.

Adrina's eyes wandered to the aged priest as he spoke. Long ago, she had stopped listening to the words he spoke, and so she figured it wasn't necessary to bow her head or close her eyes either. She told herself she would relish the day when he passed on, and then she cursed herself for thinking it. It had been Father Tenuus who had placed the crown on her father's head on coronation day. Father Tenuus who had joined her mother and father, Alexandria and Andrew, queen and king, in matrimony. And Father Tenuus who had brought her into the world.

Adrina sighed. The prayer seemed finally over. She watched attendants descend upon the tables carrying plates overloaded with fresh baked breads, platters with golden brown game hens, decanters of wine and an array of steaming dishes carrying wonderful aromas. Her mouth watered. Yet, just when everyone thought Father Tenuus would say "amen," he began to speak again.

Adrina tucked a wayward strand of dark hair behind her ear and scowled. She looked around the table. Her father, apparently midway through a smile, frowned, yet made no comment. He never did.

When Father Tenuus finally did finish, it was a mad dash to get food to the tables while it was still somewhat warm. Adrina watched in earnest as she was served. The rather pale looking man to her right, clothed in a purple velvet overcoat and blue silken shirt, turned a whiter shade of white as he raised a handkerchief to his puffy red nose. He was pretending to be aloof but Adrina knew inside he was probably seething because she was ignoring him.

King Andrew smiled as Adrina began eating without waiting for his approval. Adrina knew he liked her independent nature, for he had fostered this especially in her. Yet she also knew a great deal could be hidden in a simple smile. Its uneasy weight made her cringe and turn away from her father's gaze. Her independence was exactly what she and Lady Isador, her maternal nanny—governess—had discussed in length just the previous Seventhday.

"His Majesty is getting along in years, as am I, young Adrina," Lady Isador had told her in her frank, motherly way. "Some day you will be alone. His Majesty favors finding you a suitable mate in the near future. Already several prospective suitors have been made aware that you will soon be of courting age. His Majesty has charged me with preparing you to begin courtship. Yet, it is well known—" And this is the part that made Adrina cringe then and now, for Lady Isador had come to tears. "—that you are not a courtly lady. I am afraid I have failed miserably in my duties as your governess. I asked to be dismissed, but His Majesty wouldn't hear of it. 'She is strong willed, strong minded, not easily pleased, and quick to anger, which is perhaps my own fault,' His Majesty told me. Young Adrina, I gasped at the hearing, His Majesty is never wrong nor at fault. 'Lady Isador,' His Majesty went on to tell me, 'you have a lot of work to do if you are to retire at summer's end.' I agreed with him on that point.

"South Province is calling me home young Adrina. Only Great-Father and Mother-Earth could keep me from it. I long to see my father's house, walk amongst the great white birch trees that line the yard, and smell strong southerly breezes. Breezes that make you want to curl your toes up and walk through tall midsummer grass…"

A smile did come to Adrina's lips then, and she turned to look back at her father-king. There was a faraway look in the monarch's eyes and Adrina could only wonder as to his thoughts. Surely, he was considering the progress of the search. She had heard that not a single one of the upper lords had responded. She wagered that presently he was considering which nobles of the middle and lower houses had suitable sons.

Momentary delight came to her eyes as Chancellor Yi seemed to twitch—King Andrew had nodded ever so slightly to get his attention. No doubt having mentally completed the list, he was whispering a notation in the chancellor's time-bent ear.

Adrina played with the bit of honey-glazed hen that remained on her plate. No longer hungry, she probably could have pushed the mostly empty plate away, but soon afterwards one of the dreadful courtiers would have undoubtedly moved in and she would have been locked into a meaningless conversation. No, she thought, let them think she was interested only in eating.

When Captain Brodst, the man Adrina had nearly collided with earlier, entered and approached the king's table, Adrina's heart raced—even the captain of the guard did not interrupt the evening meal without justification. Adrina tried to listen in but could only hear some of what was being said.

"—it is urgent Your Majesty," Captain Brodst said, "a messenger has arrived this hour from the South."

King Andrew furrowed his brow. "I gather the news is more than urgent?"

Captain Brodst nodded.

"I see, have council chambers prepared. I will be along presently."

"Yes, of course, Your Majesty," said Captain Brodst, kneeling appropriately, preparing to make his exit.

"And captain?"

Captain Brodst nodded again.

"Rouse two guards to council doors."

A pained expression crossed the captain's

face. Captain Brodst took great pride in his position as captain of the king's guard and being told to do the obvious was an insult. Adrina sympathized with the burly captain. She liked him, though he seemed to have little love for her.

"At once sire," said Captain Brodst. Then he quickly departed.

Adrina was left to amble through the scattered remains on her plate. Her hope was to escape the dining hall and find a strategic position near the council chambers.

She waited, and waited, patiently thinking to herself that the matter wasn't too urgent or else her father would have departed immediately. Then again, her father had never been one quick to stir to action. Sometimes it seemed that he mulled over the simplest of decisions for hours—like the color of a new flower to put into the gardens—and then those decisions that she assumed he would deliberate over for days were made in the blink of an eye. Still, she had seen him take seven days to contemplate a heated land dispute when a decision had been desperately needed that same day to keep two of the lower lords from mauling each other.

As King Andrew laid his dinner knife aside and rinsed his fingers in the dipping bowl for what appeared to be the last time, all eyes around the great oblong table rose to greet his. The time for Adrina to make her move was now or never. She shot a withering grimace to the pale little man to her right—stay where you are, she warned with her eyes—and attempted to follow in Andrew's wake.

She glanced back as she gracefully but hurriedly exited the hall to see if anyone followed. Most of the courtiers were caught in the tangle of attendants swarming over the tables to remove the remnants of the meal. Some of the courtiers had guardedly returned to their fare as they always did. Some were already deep in meaningless conversations with whomever was to their right or left. These were the ones who had either decided they'd never gain the king's favor and it was nearly time to depart Imtal Palace, or those who were just present because it was *the* thing to do. There *were* those who had chosen the evening meal as their final battling ground—their last chance to confer with His Majesty—and these were the ones that sought to follow but were caught in the tangle of attendants.

There were also those whose task it was to watch. They were the eyes and ears of many a lord and even the paid spies of other kings. Adrina was suddenly sure the rather pale looking man beside her was not only pretending to be aloof but was also listening to the King's every word. He did not get caught up in the tangle of attendants. In fact, he moved rather adroitly through the crowded room and into the adjacent hall.

As she reached the wide open-aired corridor connecting the central wing of the castle with the West wing, Adrina's heart and mind began to race with the possibility of excitement ahead.

"A messenger with grave news," she whispered to herself.

Change.

***

Crystalline walls mirrored Queen Mother's innermost feelings. The day held promise. Her mood was bright. The room, bright.

Walls, ceiling and floor of the modest meditation cubicle were clean-swept, and broken only by the frame of the door before her. The chamber, designed for ascetic purposes, was meant to hold no distractions.

Queen Mother herself was outfitted in a flowing white robe. It too was without adornment, designed to hold no distractions. It dangled several feet beneath her crossed legs and levitated form. Her arms were also crossed. Her eyes, appropriately closed. Her head, level and directed toward the closed door. Her thoughts dwelled solely on cleansing meditation.

She did not respond to the soft summons the first time it entered her mind. Instead, she held persistently to her meditation. She was trying to forget.

My queen… came whispered words into her mind a second time.

A second time Queen Mother cast them away. She didn't want anything to spoil her pleasant mood, especially as troubled as her mind had been upon waking and considering how long it had taken her to soothe those troubles away. The day held promise, she reminded herself.

My queen… the voice came more urgently.

Annoyed now, Queen Mother opened her eyes. A light wave of her hand stirred the cubicle's door and swept it quickly open. *Do come in Brother Liyan… What brings First Counsel to my door?*

Following the unspoken whisper, the timeworn elder outfitted all in gray entered the room—the gray of the robe was a symbol of office, unlike the white of Queen Mother's robe, which was a symbol of her whims. Brother Liyan nodded to the Red Brother who stood watch just inside the chamber. Dark brown eyes regarded him for a moment and a chill ran the length of his spine.

The crystalline walls slowly adjusted to reflect agitation. At first they dulled and darkened to a metallic bronze and then settled on a murky brown. Taking note of the falling and deepening of the cubicle's glow, Brother Liyan turned pale.

My queen, Brother Liyan said as he stepped across the threshold. He kneeled appropriately, and awaited her response to make further comment. Under other circumstances, he would not have been so formal and formality would have been the last thing expected of him, but here in the halls of Sanctuary when Queen Mother herself had called a retreat it was expected of him and so he did his part.

Queen Mother responded again, only with feelings as she often did when annoyed.

Brother Liyan looked up into Queen Mother's eyes and uneasily rose from his knees. *My queen, a thousand pardons for the interruption, but this matter is urgent. You did not address it directly during the assembly, but I gather that Brother Seth prepares for the journey?*

Yes, that is so.

I do not understand. Why Brother Seth, First of the Red? His strength is needed here in Leklorall, especially now.

Queen Mother held her position, her long white dress cascading to the clean, cold floor. *It must be.*

You yourself said the chosen wouldn't survive the ordeal. The chosen will never return to East Reach… Brother Seth must not go. Who would protect in his stead? Surely then… Brother Liyan paused and looked to the brooding figure standing beside the door. *As the second, Brother Galan must stay…*

That is a truth you would do well never to impart again… Only those of the assembly know the fate of the chosen… Brother Seth is free to choose as many Brothers of the Red as he feels necessary to accompany him. If it is in his will to choose Brother Galan, then she too must go.

Brother Liyan paled visibly again, yet would make the protest he had repeated over and over in his thoughts in preparation for this very moment. *My queen, have you considered what it is you do? The Red are your chosen protectors. It will soon be too late to—*

Shielding their thoughts and slamming the cubicle's door abruptly, Queen Mother didn't allow Brother Liyan to finish. Black walls mirrored her increasingly somber mood, for these were the very thoughts she had sought to cleanse away through her meditation. *Precisely,* was her response and the Brother Liyan's eyes went wide.

My queen... Brother Liyan didn't understand.

Good Brother, savor this feeling on a future day, but for now know that I am fully cognizant of my actions. I am the living prophet of my people, am I not? I know very well what it is I do... If I as Queen Mother, the heart and soul of my people, cannot pay the dearest of prices for the ridding of the greatest of ailments, then I, and all, fail the greatest of tests... Brother Seth is our only hope. He will fight to survive where others would surely succumb. Never have I seen such faith. Never have I seen such determination. He must believe he can succeed. And he must truly strive for this.

My queen, Brother Liyan gasped. *I truly did not know or understand, forgive me.*

There is no need for forgiveness. There is nothing to forgive. We each have our parts in this and we must play them out. We have waited too long to act. Sathar has the ear of King Mark. Our people return to the lands of Man... There was evident sadness in her voice.

Brother Galan, called out Queen Mother.

Galan opened her brown eyes and cleared her thoughts. *Queen Mother?*

Leave us now. Tell Brother Seth I await his presence...

Galan fixed her eyes upon Brother Liyan. Remember your place, her deep-probing stare said. Then she quickly departed the chamber.

***

Out of breath from the long run, Vilmos doubled over. The sharp pain in his sides told him the run had been especially good. The way he figured it, if the walk from his father's house to the edge of the woods took thirty minutes one way and he ran it in five, he had nearly an hour to do whatever he pleased.

After the pain and the spots before his eyes passed, Vilmos quickly stretched. He knew from experience if his leg muscles were too tense or if he strained a muscle, he'd have to walk—or limp—home. Upon finishing, he put on his boots. He preferred to run barefoot; otherwise, the boots gave him blisters.

The air grew suddenly cold as an icy wind howled up the little country path that parted the dark wood. It was then that Vilmos noticed how quiet the woods were that morning.

He stared long into the dark wood—keeper of his secrets—as he often did. Here his childhood dreams had been realized. In the shadow of the great trees, he could run screaming as loud as he pleased, slay fire-breathing dragons by the score, discover incredible lost treasures, play with imaginary friends, and still return home on time—well, usually.

Vilmos easily collected a large bundle of light wood from the nearby thicket, and then laid it aside. The wind howled. He stared up the overgrown path. He never ventured very far into the woods—only far enough to be within their shadows, yet close enough to still see the sunlight of the clearing beyond.

He heard what sounded like footsteps. He turned and stared, but saw only shadows. An alarm went off in his mind. He picked up a large branch and wielded it before him.

"Hello?" he called out, "Is someone there?"

Movement in the shadows caught his eye. For an instant, he could have sworn he saw an old man carrying a gnarled cane.

"Hel-lo?"

Holding the stick before him, in what to him seemed a menacing pose, Vilmos crept into the shadows of the dark woods. Leaves crunched beneath his boots. He grimaced. Movement caught his careful eye again. He turned, raising the stick, ready to strike, then stopped cold. He saw a mound of black fur and dark eyes, a great black bear, kin of the much smaller browns the village huntsmen often sought.

The giant bear was no more than five feet away.

Two days ago in Olex Village, one of the three villages in their cluster, a young girl had been mauled to death by a bear. Vilmos didn't want to share her fate. He stood perfectly still, his heart racing so fast it seemed to want to jump out of his chest. Then the great beast reared up on its hind legs. Terror gripped Vilmos' mind. Warm urine raced down his legs. His every thought told him to run, but he couldn't. It was as if he was frozen to the spot where he stood.

His eyes bulging, he stared at the bear, sure any moment it would swing one of its mighty paws and that would be the end of it. He didn't want to die; he had so many dreams left unfulfilled.

Again, a voice in his mind screamed, Run! But he could not.

Images from his nightmare became real. In the nightmare, the dark priests had come for him and, like now, he had been unable to run. In the dream, blue flames conjured from his fright and desperation had lashed out at the priests. The priests had merely laughed and still they had taken him.

As if conjured again from his fear and desperation, the forbidden magic came. Vilmos felt a prickling sensation—raw energy—in his fingertips. In his mind, he screamed No! at himself and the bear. What if this was the one time too many? What if this was the time that made the dark priests come for him? Then he asked himself the final what if. What if the bear charged now?

One swipe of its powerful paw was all it would take to end his young life. The girl from Olex Village had been taken nearly so.

What *had* the village huntsmen said about bears? Had the girl not run when she should have? Or ran when she shouldn't have? Vilmos couldn't remember. He stared directly at the bear. It was sniffing the air as if insulted that it was crosswinds from him. Then suddenly it dropped to all fours—Vilmos was sure this was it, this was the end. The bear would charge, swipe and he would die.

The bear roared.

Vilmos squeezed his eyes tight. A scream built in his throat, but died as it escaped his lips.

Silence followed.

Vilmos waited—surely the great bear must be charging—and waited. The forest was deadly still. Vilmos inched one eye open, then the other. The bear was gone. Astonished, both his eyes grew wide. He stared into the shadows. Listened.

Nothing.

He sniffed the air; there was a strange scent in it. Scorched wood. Burnt flesh. Singed hair. All three?

Slowly, Vilmos edged forward until he was directly in front of one of the forest's giant oaks. He ran his hands along two still warm scorch marks in the tree's trunk. He swallowed a lump in his throat. He had done what he shouldn't have. He had conjured the blue flames.

Suddenly remembering breakfast and the woodpile, he turned his gaze to the forest's edge. He saw the sun in the clearing and ran for its safety.

***

Seth glanced at the piles of scrolls and tomes spread across his desk. No matter what Queen Mother had told him, there was no way he could remain unaffected by such writings. The fact that she wouldn't listen to his protests only served to agitate him.

Focus, Seth told himself. He set one of the leather-bound tomes before him, tried to convince himself he wanted to read it, then after a long pause opened it. The book was titled, "Courtship rituals of the noble class." He read the first page without any difficulty; it was an introduction. In fact, he waded his way through three entire chapters without any difficulty.

Yet, he wasn't expecting to find a drawing as he turned the page to chapter four. Disgusted, he pushed the book away. There was no way he would continue to study such perversity. His thoughts were cluttered, so much had happened yesterday.

He focused his thoughts on the breeze blowing outside the protected fields of Sanctuary. He raced with the swells, danced in the swirls and accompanied the currents into the heavens. There was moisture in the clouds. This was good. The rain was needed to quench the dryness of the earth.

Peace of mind swept over Seth. The will of the land found him. He pushed away the troubled thoughts of today and yesterday, and returned to the book. Hastily, he turned to the next page and began to read.

Without announcement, a figure clad in red burst into the room. Seth looked up from his studies only long enough to see it was Brother Galan. He glanced up once more to see her prepare for a bath, then his thoughts returned to the book.

You study too much. You need to relax... whispered a soft voice in his mind, *You should join me.*

Seth looked up again to see Galan standing before him. *I wish I could.*

Is it true then what I've heard? Galan sent strong emotions with the words, longing and curiosity.

For the first time as he looked at her, Seth saw Galan as different, beautiful. Suddenly uneasy and not understanding why, Seth stared down at his books. *Their strange ideas pollute my mind even now.*

Then it is true.

Seth wavered his head left and then right in acknowledgment.

Galan asked, *What do you find most odd about them?*

Seth smiled. Galan had the insatiable curiosity of a preborn child. She held the same view of looking at the world. She saw things as flashes of colors and feelings. Only Galan would ask what he found most odd about them. *I find them most odd. Everything about them. This notion of marriage. Their idea of distinct gender. Their class structure. They would find me calling you, Brother, very odd.*

Why is that? Galan scratched at her side. *Why has Queen Mother told you to study their ways?*

Will you stand my watch again this day?

Galan answered not with words, but with feelings, playfulness.

There *were* times Seth could easily forget Galan had only recently ascended. At times like now, however, he was painfully aware of it. Galan had many seasons of maturing ahead. Yet, Seth also knew that beneath the facade of youth lurked a mind that was quick and strong, already nearly a match for his own—which when he had ascended had also been advanced. In twelve short seasons, Galan had become the second highest of the Red Order.

Galan sent him impatience.

Seth shook his head again. *All right, all right, I'll join you... One hour away from my studies will do more good than harm.*

Chapters 1 and 2: Review Questions

1. Why is Princess Adrina sad at the beginning of the story?
___
___
___

2. Why is it important that Vilmos learn how to listen carefully to others?
___
___
___

3. What does Seth learn from Queen Mother as they walk to Sanctuary's High Hall that startles him?
___
___
___

4. Why does King Andrew tell Princess Adrina "Only so, dear Adrina. Only so," and what does he mean?
___
___
___

5. What's so important about the messenger's arrival during the evening meal?
___
___

6. Why is Queen Mother upset when she talks with Brother Liyan?
___
___
___

7. What happens when Vilmos meets the bear in the forest?
___
___
___

8. What does Seth mean by these statements: Galan had the insatiable curiosity of a preborn child. She held the same view of looking at the world. She saw things as flashes of color and feelings. Only Galan would ask what he found most odd about them [men].
___
___
___

Words to Watch

Occurrence	Retribution	Merciless
Oscillate	Perplex	Befuddlement
Eavesdrop	Permeate	Injustice
Breach	Defiance	Aimlessly
Ethics	Malice	Adolescence
Accompany	Preordained	Insignia
Prescient	Encounter	Spontaneous
Unwholesome	Temptation	
Intuitive	Perish	

Chapter Three: It Begins

Days passed. News of the messenger from the Far South spread throughout Imtal Palace. Word in the halls was that it had been a personal message from King Charles of Sever. Something was terribly wrong in the small Kingdom of Sever, though none knew what it was. To Adrina it seemed servants knew more about the visit than she did. She had always been adept at gathering bits of information and tying them together, finding connections between the smallest of occurrences when there seemed none, which gave her enormous pleasure—a small triumph in an otherwise gray, boring world. She had truly done her best to listen outside the chamber doors, but had not succeeded.

Now it seemed she had a second chance. She was sure another messenger had just arrived. The palace heralds had just sounded in greeting, and minutes earlier she had heard the outer city heralds' trumpeting calls. Adrina glanced at the flowing blue gown Lady Isador was still in the process of hemming—Lady Isador wouldn't hear of allowing a servant to do the work. "Proper hands do proper work," she had said and chased the servants away. That had been hours ago. It was now well past midday.

The clatter of hooves against the stones of the outer courtyard caused Adrina to jump and turn.

"Stand still, Young Highness," said Lady Isador. "Look, look what I've done. I have to begin again."

Still on her tiptoes, Adrina stared long. The sight of a sweated mount passing to the stables brought despair to her face. If she didn't hurry she might never find out if she was right about the messenger. Think quickly, she told herself, think quickly.

"Down, down, down my dear," said Lady Isador, "no wonder that hem looked all wrong. Mustn't stand on tiptoes."

Isador stopped her work and looked up at Adrina. "Oh, child, you look definitely peaked. Are you hungry? The day is long. Shall I order the mid-day meal?"

"Could we finish this tomorrow, Lady Isador?"

"Sixthday is only a few days away. We wouldn't want to disappoint his lordship, the son of Klaive, would we?"

Adrina rose to her tiptoes again and turned a longing stare toward the stables.

"There goes that hem again," muttered Lady Isador. "My eyes aren't what they used to be, perhaps they do need a rest."

Adrina asked, "Is that a yes?"

"Yes, Young Highness, it is."

***

Seth returned from the bath to find Brother Everrelle waiting for him. *Queen Mother wishes you to High Hall and would have you wait in the antechamber until her summons to enter,* Everrelle said, and Seth rushed off.

Seth found the antechamber empty. He waited, his thoughts filling with dread. Hours passed.

The walls of the antechamber oscillated through casts of gray, hovering just slight of brilliant silver, then fading to a quasi-black. Oblivious to this light show playing out before his eyes, Seth sulked. He had seen it a thousand times before and would probably see it many thousands more. The subtle but swift changes were supposed to be soothing, but he wasn't soothed.

Seth felt utterly helpless as he waited. He considered eavesdropping on those behind the closed doors. It would have been easy enough to do, a simple projecting of thoughts, nothing more. Those within would not have gone to the trouble of masking open thoughts, for the chambers did that for them. That was what the adjoining chambers had been designed for. Thoughts were enclosed within the sanctioned walls and went no further. The antechamber was considered part of the hall. There was another such chamber at the northern end. Guests could be seated in either of these chambers, and often were, and thoughts needed to pass back and forth freely. So no, the thoughts would not have been blocked to Seth. He would have only to reach out to them. Yet he did not do this for it would have breached the bounds of ethics ingrained into him since birth. He would wait and bide his time.

Seth turned his thoughts to Galan now. As they had walked to the bathing pool, distress had replaced her playfulness. Later, she had told him of Brother Liyan's visit yesterday. Afterward she told him she had not masked her thoughts during their conversation. She had heard, seen and felt everything.

I am afraid for you my brother, but I must not say why... Galan had said. *Will you promise to return to the chamber afterward?*

Seth had said he would.

Seth's thoughts became unfocused for a time. Then just when Seth thought he could wait no more, the doors swung open and the summons came.

He was shocked to see that all the members of the three councils attended and that many others streamed in through the far door. Many eyes were directed at him now and he did not know why.

There was an unusual amount of energy in the air accompanied by a strange silence, which to his prescient mind was like an unwholesome numbing. People fidgeted around in their cushioned seats or floated just above them nervously but voiced no thoughts.

Seth was beckoned to the fore, not by the flow of words or feelings to his wildly spinning mind but by the briefest stroking of his intuitive senses, a presage bundled in the form of a picture and thrust upon his mind, which was done for effect. It was such an overpowering tool that only Queen Mother would have ever resorted to its use, for any other would have provoked open wrath in the recipient and retribution would have been called for. Sure, Queen Mother could have sent simple thoughts of hot–cold and thus directed him, but any child could have done that. She wanted to stun him, and she had.

Head slightly lowered, eyes wide and upturned, Seth lurched to a perplexed halt. Words whisked through his mind as through a dream and he heard only a part of the message.

... I send my chosen protectors to return to the lands of Man as a symbol of my resolve...

Then suddenly an avalanche of voices cascaded into his head as Queen Mother's words spawned a heated debate. Seth could only stare blankly ahead, still half in stupor as he sought to digest the multiple conversations.

Queen Mother lowered her gaze and when their eyes met a smile passed her lips—only in that instant, did Seth realize that none of the others knew what she had done to him. She had in a way stolen the words from his thoughts before he could offer protest. When he finally did come to protest it was already too late, only Seth had the misfortune of not realizing it then. He began his protest.

How can this be so? he demanded, *Surely this is some sort of…*

"Brother Seth, the decision of the High Council is final as is the word of Queen Mother," the voice that permeated the air of the great hall was Brother Liyan's. It was not often that one of the Brotherhood spoke aloud, but this too was done for effect. Immediate silence followed.

"But I must stay here. Here is where I belong. I have sworn to the Father to protect. Send another. The Red's first duty is to protect Queen Mother."

"No, Brother Seth," the voice again spoken aloud this time was Queen Mother's and now audible gasps crisscrossed the chamber. Queen Mother never spoke aloud. "It was I who offered your services. The Brotherhood shall serve in this undertaking. It was I, who said the Red would be the chosen ones."

What of the Brown? Is this not a duty of the warrior order? Seth was just as purposeful when he responded in thought as when Queen Mother had spoken aloud. It was a small defiance, yes, but it was a defiance far greater than offering his opinion when she had obviously warned him that she wanted to hear little more than silence from him.

The presage had been her warning to him and now Seth had defied her, yet those of the council were not privy to her earlier act. So while gasps audible and inaudible—those of the mind—passed around the chamber again, Queen Mother fixed her open gaze upon him again. Under the weight of her stare he must hold his tongue, or suffer the accompanying wrath.

"Brother Seth, their part will come. It is not now." Queen Mother again spoke aloud. "Why do you think you have been studying their ways these many past weeks?"

It is our duty, my duty, to stay. I will not go… Seth closed his mind to further thought. He did not wish to listen to any more nonsense. He had sworn with his life's last thread that he would protect Queen Mother for all times. He would not leave her now or ever.

There was a trace of anger in Queen Mother's countenance and the naked rendering of such a strong emotion in the company of the Council and so many others was in itself significant enough to send Seth's knees to trembling. It wasn't that he feared her wrath. Queen Mother held no malice within her—her eyes held only caring and her heart only love. There was greater pain than physical pain and the greatest mental anguish to his kind was shame and dishonor.

Seth? Brother Ry'al of the Blue thrust the word into his mind.

Seth refused to open his thoughts.

Still the stubborn one aren't you. Seth the protector. Can you not see? Surely, you must see it. The time is upon us. All is up to you, chastised Ry'al.

All this from Seth's final refusal to Ry'al's final entreaty occurred between one heartbeat and the next—the speed of pure thought.

If I must use my rank of office on you, I will. It is as it must be; no others could make the journey. What lies ahead is preordained for you , said Brother Liyan, *whether you want to believe it or not, you know in your heart it is the truth.*

The force of Liyan's thoughts thrust into his mind confounded Seth and nearly sent a wave of anger rushing over him—yet he was able to turn that anger to his advantage. "I see the truth of your words, Brother Liyan of the Grey, Queen's Counsel, greatest of the wise." Seth spoke aloud, the precise phrasing of his words brought a partial smile to Liyan's face.

"I make formal apology to High Council and to Queen Mother, who is the heart and soul of her people and who has wisdom second to no living mortal."

Now Brother Liyan's smile blossomed and broadened—this naked emotion was allowed. *Wise words,* he sent to Seth alone.

Seth turned to face the Council, waiting for acceptance of the apology.

Council accepts your apology, Brother Seth of the Red...

Relief passed over Seth, though the most important expression of forgiveness had not been passed yet—Queen Mother had not spoken. This never came, though Seth waited for what seemed an eternity in his turbulent thoughts.

Who will accompany me? Seth asked, breaking the silence.

I shall leave the choices up to you, Brother Seth. The voice in his mind was that of Queen Mother. *I know it will be a difficult one but I have confidence in you, Brother Seth of the Red, first of that order, Queen's Protector. You are the chosen one.*

***

After piling the light wood cleanly on the floor next to the wood stack, Vilmos crossed to his room and changed clothes, heedless of the fixed scowl aimed directly at him. He was tardy, but only barely so. During the tangle with the bear he had lost the rope to tie around the bundle of wood. Instead of running home with a neatly tied bundle over his shoulder, he had had to walk. The walk hadn't bothered him though; his legs had been shaky and unsteady after the encounter.

His eyes wide, Vilmos told his mother of the encounter with the bear and later about his inadvertent use of the forbidden magic. Lillath's face turned white with horror. She swept Vilmos up in her arms.

"You poor, poor dear, frightened to death like that."

Vilmos' father put aside the Great Book and directed angry eyes at him. "Bear or no bear, there is no excuse for magic."

"Yes, father, I know, but the power just comes to me. I can do nothing to stop it."

Despite a mother's pleading eyes, the angry words continued. "No excuses. If you had returned after gathering the wood, you never would've encountered the bear. You must resist the temptation to use the forbidden. It is the work of evil. You will spread it to the land and you will be damned!"

"Now don't be harsh on the child, Vil." Lillath called her husband Vil to keep words directed at father and son separate. "Go ahead, Vilmos, eat, you look beyond starved." The objection finally said, the woman returned to her meal.

Vilmos started to smile, a flicker of hope that was cut short.

"I'm not being harsh. Do you want them to come? Do you want them to take him away?"

Vilmos gritted his teeth; here came the lesson.

"Salamander dweller amidst flames; Sylph light and dainty as air; Elf of forest and water; Gnome under mountain and stone; inhabitants of the four elements no more. All because Queen of Elves took pity on Gnome and so wed King of Gnomes under Solstice Mountain. Unknowingly she brought with her the gift of Elf magic. Elf magic in the hands of Gnome—pure evil.

"Sylph, Salamander, Elf and Gnome, no

more. Only the four offspring of King Gnome and Queen Elf survived. Naiad dweller of river and spring. Nereid dweller of sea. Oread dweller under mountain. Elf dweller of forest. In the end, even though they fought the evil of this new magic and directed it toward good ends, all perished save willful Elf who was in the end washed into the sea with her people. This is the lore of the Four Peoples. Go now. Contemplate this lesson and the error of your ways."

Cheerless eyes of a worried mother silently followed Vilmos. He could feel her eyes upon his back. He retreated to the sanctuary of his room where he began a vigilant watch of the ceiling. He supposed that made it look like he was contemplating the error of his ways, but in truth he hated his studies.

A long time passed before his mother entered the room, carrying with her a large tome, the Great Book, and a plate full with breakfast foods: still-warm black bread, honey cakes, country jams, dark yellow cheeses and three varieties of smoked sausages. She sat the plate down and began to read from the Great Book.

Vilmos only half listened.

"After He was cast from our world, those among us, the wise, foretold that someday He would return. If we allow him to escape the darkness through our use of magic, He will survive the endless journey of darkness… Magic draws upon the threads of the whole of the world. Eventually the threads will unravel. A rift will be created. When He has finally regained his powers, He will use this rift…"

Such teachings had been lectured many times before and though they were not lost on him, Vilmos didn't give them much thought. The Dark Lord had perished a millennia ago. How could he return by the simple use of magic? Besides, there seemed a never-ending list of lessons pertaining to the use of magic. It was true that tales of the Dark Lord and Queen Elf were the two that he heard constantly, but he was tired of them all.

"I try hard not to use it, mother, but I slip on occasion."

"The use of the magic is expressly forbidden. Never use it. Do you understand me? Never."

Vilmos appealed to her with his innocent eyes.

"I know but the power just comes to me. It is growing stronger, mother."

A look of shock spread across Lillath's features. She gasped. "You must not use it. Vilmos, promise me."

"I can do nothing to stop it."

Lillath, now appearing older than her years, swept Vilmos up in her arms. She held him for a time in a motherly embrace, and then let him go. She knelt beside him and placed both hands on his cheeks.

"After He was cast from our world those among us, the wise, foretold that someday He would return, but only if we continued to use magic. Magic is evil, Vilmos. This is why you must never use it. Promise me." Her voice had never sounded grimmer.

"I will try, mother."

Overtures of desperation, also a hint of vast knowledge, touched her words now. "Even I could not stop what must be done if you don't do as I ask. Soon, mind you. Do you understand?"

"You wouldn't let them take me away, would you, mother?"

"No, I would never allow the priests to take you away, Vilmos. I promise." Lillath was crying now and on those words she returned to her kitchen.

In his heart Vilmos believed her. She wouldn't let them take him away, yet if they came he knew she would have no choice. They would take him away. He would never see the Kingdom of Sever again.

Vivid images from the nightmare returned to his mind and with them came clouded, troubled thoughts. He did not want to be taken away from his home. He did not want to go away. He did not want to leave his mother. He loved Lillath desperately. She was all he had.

Vilmos closed his eyes then escaped to the place he went when troubled. A deep, majestic valley spread before him. Its view was breathtaking as he stared down into its depths, imagining himself a great, giant eagle lazily circling high above the valley floor. This was his special place, *only* his, he thought. He was the great winged beast, master of all it surveyed, who could swoop, soar and dive to the valley floor or glide up on a light puff of air.

Alone and free, the great golden eagle flew.

Vilmos had always been different from other children. His powers separated him and he knew and understood this as bitter reality. Other children wouldn't play with him. He was an outcast, and he had been ever since the fateful day he had mistakenly loosed his magic during Three Village Day two summer's ago.

A tear rolled down his cheek. The blue flames were the cause of all his anguish. Two summer's ago he had nearly killed Willig of Olex Village. Over a game of catch-and-seek, the big boy had pinned him down and had beaten him mercilessly—Willig was a poor loser. Vilmos had used his only means of protection and now he was cast out, alone, forsaken by all—except by Lillath who loved him with a mother's devotion.

He didn't care, thought Vilmos, as he soared above the valley. He knew who he was. He was himself and that was all that mattered. Besides, now he didn't have to go to those silly celebrations and he no longer had to take lessons with Willig or Erik, the other counselors' sons,

either. His father had hired private tutors to continue his education—a difficult undertaking since there were few in the land that could read or write with much skill.

A mocking grin broke the internal corners of his mind. Temporarily the image of the great eagle and the valley faded. Many tutors had come and gone since that terrible day. Yet his current teacher, Midori, was warm and generous. She did not overtax him with studies like the others. And although Vilmos did like her, he still had tried to frighten her away with his use of magic, as he had those before her. He had even resorted to his most resourceful trick—levitation: the floating of objects. The prank had only brought laughter and was ignored, to his utter dismay and befuddlement.

Devious thoughts clustered in his mind—scaring off another teacher would surely even out the score with his father. The frustration on Vil's face would suffice as repayment for many chastisements—besides, it had taken a long time to find this newest teacher. He would use the blue flames, the blue flames that he had unleashed upon the unsuspecting boy, the blue flames that scorched and decimated, the blue flames that stemmed from his anger. He allowed the thought to settle upon his mind in a fanciful way.

However, the tutor had been so kind to him. It suddenly seemed an injustice to think such thoughts about her. Could he really hurt her? he wondered.

She was unlike any other teacher he had ever had. In fact, he usually enjoyed her visits very much. With effort, the thoughts slipped away before the anger that would sweep him away found him.

The transition back to the valley was made with a single folding of thoughts one on top of the other. The eagle with its stout, generous wings soared above the pristine valley. Floating on a pleasant pocket of air, sinking to the valley floor, scouring for prey, it filled Vilmos with life.

Vilmos did not know that in this form he also breathed life into a creature nearly as old as the valley itself.

***

Brother Liyan closed his eyes and listened to Seth's tale. After the council meeting Brother Seth had wandered the halls aimlessly and caught himself from time to time staring down from above his own thoughts as if he were aloof from them, and during one such time he remembered Brother Galan. She had been waiting for him since early afternoon.

Seth returned to the room they shared then and did a thing he claimed not to understand. Galan was sitting on the edge of her bed, running a comb through her long hair. He sat beside her and the next thing he knew his lips were pressed against hers.

Immediately afterward, Seth fled the room and in his confused state of mind, said he knew of only one person he could turn to. Brother Liyan had been meditating in his private chambers and, without announcement, Seth burst into the room and in one great rush of thoughts explained all that had happened since he left the hall.

Liyan opened his eyes. *Brother Seth, you have hardly committed an unforgivable transgression.*

Seth sent Liyan tortured thoughts. *These ideals of Man corrupt my thinking.*

Brother Liyan had been Seth's mentor for only one season now, his appointment at Queen Mother's request. Just now he understood what it must have been like enduring the teachings of the seven orders and after every phase of the training beginning anew like a child and always in training with children. He was suddenly less afraid of the mysterious and powerful Red. *It is Mother-Earth herself that corrupts your thinking... Have you never been beyond Kapital or Sanctuary?*

I have traveled the canals of the city from end to end with Sailmaster Cagan, and I have traveled the road to Sanctuary. Is there anything beyond that I would care to see?

It seemed that Brother Liyan also understood why Seth had fought so hard in High Hall. Seth was genuinely afraid of venturing into the world and Liyan had perhaps discovered the one thing that could bring true fear to one of the Red. *The whole of the world, Brother Seth, the whole of the world. Sights so marvelous you could hardly begin to imagine them all. And never forget that what you call Kapital, the people call Leklorall.*

Liyan sent Seth a mental image, the green of a forest against the backdrop of a white-capped mountain, the sky so blue it was almost purple. *That is our ancient home. Is it not truly beautiful?*

What of my act? Is my mind perverted?

I should think so, said Liyan, quickly adding before Seth could fly into a panic, *but I do think it is treatable.*

I am being serious and you mock me?

Brother Seth, I will tell you a secret I have never told another. Liyan paused and collected his thoughts. Tears came to his eyes, for now he also understood why Queen Mother had appointed him as Seth's mentor. *Just as you fear what you do not know, the unknown in the world, I have always feared the Brothers of the Red. In fact, terror is a better word to describe the emotion—*

That is an emotion we are trained to evoke.

That explains much, but it is not the point I am trying to make. We all have our fears, and what we fear most is a thing unknown to us. From birth, your kind is secreted away from all of society. By the time you complete your training you are passed youthful adolescence and then we dub you protectors of Queen Mother, never thinking that up until now all your dealings have been with teachers and children.

You were wrong about the Brown Order. They were the chosen warriors only out of necessity. Before the Brown there was always the Red and, since the establishment of the Brown during those dark centuries when brother turned against brother, the Red are still, first and foremost, the warrior-protectors of Queen and people.

Perhaps it is a good thing that Queen Mother wishes you out into the world, and a good thing you studied the ways of Man. Their culture is not so different from our own that you could not learn from it. Liyan paused, though just for a moment. *With Elfkind mating instinct often skips generations for reasons only Great-Father and Mother-Earth truly understand. Your feelings are not wrong Seth; they are as natural as wind.*

With Brother Galan, I would suggest you follow your instincts, perhaps it will bring good. There is however, one thing you should know, these feelings may never find her… It is one of the tragedies of our kind. For now, you should turn your thoughts on the journey ahead— Brother Liyan put a hand on Seth's shoulder. *—Are you prepared to greet the world? Is the world ready for you?*

***

Adrina still harbored hopes that a messenger had arrived from the Far South. Her father hadn't been in the study, nor had she seen Chancellor Yi—both sure signs something was afoot. She raced down the hall, down a stairway, along a set of corridors, and then stopped. As she ducked into the shadows of the hall, she covered her mouth to muffle a squeal of glee. Guards were outside her father's private council chambers.

The door opened. A lithe figure entered the hall and darted away—a messenger. He bore Kingdom insignia; no doubt, he carried a response to the message King Andrew must have just received. Minutes later, a second figure entered the hall—small-statured and obviously fatigued. Adrina watched him pass. He bore no insignia save one on the upturned collar of the cloak draped over his arm. It had white and gold bands—a king's messenger.

Adrina came out of seclusion in the shadows, wandered past the closed chamber doors and tossed a wink to one of the guards standing without. She knew they listened—even when they knew they shouldn't. She also knew how to make most of them talk, especially the younger man on the right. A number of ways to touch his heart and stir his tongue crossed her mind. Perhaps she would use some of the ploys and deceptive promises she had so recently been taught.

"No man can resist your eyes," she whispered to herself as the words echoed in her mind.

Another wink delivered, Adrina meandered up the nearby spiral stair. She knew where she would find that particular young guardsman later. It was to this place that she went, intent on waiting.

She stared down into the deadly stillness of the garden from the balcony where she waited. She had once imagined it contained all the colors of the world, though not now—now it seemed just as dead as everything else around her. Queen Alexandria, her mother, had put the array of gardens together, flower by flower, into one great garden. Now she too was dead: a victim of the cold, uncaring death that shrouded Imtal Proper.

Adrina paced as she waited and chuckled to herself about the pompous little courtier in his purple velvet overcoat and blue silken shirt. He was still attending dinners in the great hall, and still lent an ear to the king's every word. She laughed at him because she hurt and because there were small tears welling up in her eyes. She laughed until the pain went away and then she laughed a little bit more because the laughter sounded good in her ears.

The sun had already set by the time the young guardsman approached and the tears were long gone. Adrina waited until he passed her and then tossed a well-timed girlish giggle into the air, only then stepping from the shadows.

"Your turn at watch at an end so soon?" she asked.

"Your Highness, you know it is," said a mild voice, "sunrise and sunset are the times of the changing of the guard."

"Guardsman Emel," Adrina said several times. She said this to slight him, and Emel knew this very well, just as he knew they had been friends practically since birth. This was her way of reminding him of his place and also reminding him that he had something she wanted.

"Acting Sergeant," he said, "now if you'll excuse me—"

Obviously, he was still angry with her for what she had done to him and in a way, Adrina didn't blame him.

"—Acting Sergeant Emel, who'd've guessed?"

Emel's pace quickened. "Just until Sergeant Stytt's group returns from the Free City."

"From Solntse?" inquired Adrina, "Really from Solntse?"

She collected herself, recovering skillfully her slip in composure. "I could see to it that he is re-positioned there permanently."

She threw the offering at him, hoping he would pounce on it.

Emel deliberately chased away a spark of awe from his face. He could still and quite vividly recall what had happened the last time he had told her things he shouldn't have. Yet, he couldn't help wondering if she really could do what she proposed.

"What do you want in return?" he asked.

"Information, that's all."

Emel had his own skill of tongue and he knew the exact words to pull Adrina in and seal the offering. She would not get the best of him this time. "Something about *trouble*, though I'm not exactly sure what. You know how hard it is to hear anything through those damnable stones…"

Adrina thoughts swirled. She quickly equated trouble with excitement. She linked her arm in Emel's and pulled him to the edge of the balcony, saying nothing until she hid her glee.

"Geoffrey of Solntse owes me a debt, did I ever tell you that?"

"What kind of debt?" Emel called her bluff. He wouldn't fall for her lies anymore, as he had so many times in the past. He was now an acting sergeant. He must behave accordingly.

"Well, ah… ah," began Adrina, stumbling, stuttering, at a temporary loss for words, "a passed down one, actually. One really owed to the crown prince, one he must repay out of duty… and gratitude."

At his hesitation, she directed probing eyes—it could have been the truth.

Emel didn't believe her, but he did find it hard to be cross with her, especially when she was so close to him. He could feel her warmth. He missed the friendship they'd had, but he'd never admit it.

"There is a squabble in the *Minors* again." Emel used a double-edged slang for the four lesser kingdoms.

Adrina's eyes went wide. She tightened the link of their arms, pulling him a little closer.

"Between Sever and Vostok," added Emel, setting his own hook.

"*Again?*" asked Adrina, "Really?"

"King Peter stepped in… but… that's all I know. I could hear no more." Emel broke off intentionally.

"Emel, I'm sorry, really and truly sorry. I shouldn't have let you take all the blame before. I shouldn't have let your father send you away to High Road. I missed you the whole of last winter and into spring. I've wanted to talk to you since your return, but, but—Oh, if you know anything more, anything at all, you have to tell me. I'm going to die, just shrivel up and die, if I have to remain here in this boredom."

Adrina paused as her face flooded with emotion.

"Please."

Emel pulled away from her.

"Fair-weather friend," he shouted back as he stormed away.

"Emel, please don't leave. By the Mother, I missed you."

Hearing this, Emel hesitantly turned to look back at her, a thing he shouldn't have done. He couldn't wander long in her eyes without giving in to her desires.

Adrina repeated her plea and Emel swallowed a bit of his pride. "If I tell you the rest of what I know, do you promise to tell no one and can I rely on your word and swear you to secrecy?"

Adrina nodded.

"No, I want to hear you say it."

"I promise Emel, I will tell no one."

"Not *even* the Lady Isador?"

"Not *even* Lady Isador."

"Remember your promise, and that you are only as good as your word." Emel was hesitant to say more, but he began again just the same. "The rumors of unrest are true. I mean *really* true."

He was excited now and did nothing to hide it.

"King Jarom is supposedly behind it all, that is according to that page of King Charles, if you can believe him. He seemed the trustworthy type though. Yet, his kingdom is at stake. Quashan' garrison is to be roused to full alert status. Can you believe it? I'd give anything be in South Province now. Wow!

"That's it though, I don't know any more. I could get into *real* trouble for telling you this."

"I will tell no one," Adrina said, hiding hints of elation in a steady tone.

Emel eyed her.

"*Really*, I will tell no one, you have my word."

Adrina touched a spontaneous kiss to Emel's cheek and walked away, extremely pleased with herself. She tidied this away with rumors of the Bandit Kingdom's insurgencies around the northern borderlands—proof again that life beyond Imtal was *exciting* and *vibrant*. She knew enough about the Alliance of Kingdoms to know that the chances of war were slim, but some good strife always mixed things up a bit. Attendance of court would be more exciting if she knew angry words were going to flare. The bitter place in King Jarom's mouth for the Great Kingdom was well known and goading this along would bring her distinct pleasure, if given the chance. She wouldn't let it get too far though, just enough to stir things up. It was about time that Andrew showed the Minors to their proper place.

Adrina descended a long flowing stairway that lead down into the central gardens and moved along its paths without seeing much of what she passed. When she reached the far end, Adrina stopped for a moment and looked back toward the upper balcony. Barely visible amidst the deepening shadows was a single figure bent over the railing with arms crossed. Adrina knew it was Emel and she paused for a moment more. The conversation they had just had hadn't been a conversation between good friends. She had always intended to make up for what she had done to him, but the time had never seemed right.

Feeling tired, the day at an end, Adrina returned to her chambers where she was sure Lady Isador waited. Having avoided the old woman all day, she could endure just about anything right now.

Chapter 3: Word Sort

Can you rewrite the word list in alphabetical order? Hint: A to Z.

Occurrence
Oscillate
Eavesdrop
Breach
Ethics
Accompany
Prescient
Unwholesome
Intuitive

Can you rewrite the word list in alphabetical order? Hint: A to Z.

Retribution
Perplex
Permeate
Defiance
Malice
Preordained
Encounter
Temptation
Perish

Can you rewrite the word list in reverse alphabetical order? Hint: Z to A.

Merciless
Befuddlement
Injustice
Aimlessly
Adolescence
Insignia
Spontaneous

Words to Watch

Plague	Discount
Endearing	Perfunctory
Baritone	Melodramatic
Mysterious	Competition
Reverent	Standards
Defensive	Pristine
Etiquette	Judgment

Chapter Four: Discovery

Imtal palace held an unusual silence even for the late hour of the night. Adrina tossed and turned, enduring a fitful dream from which she had awoken more than once. Dreams had descended upon her normally soft world of slumber of late—one in particular had plagued her sleep for many weeks, though she told no one. On this particular night voices in the hall passing her door wrested her from sleep. The old chancellor with his coughs and sneezes—which at one time she had thought of as endearing, though not now—was the next to pass, followed by the low, baritone moaning of Father Tenuus.

"Sire, please wake," called out Chancellor Yi with much reverence, "Keeper Martin wishes to speak with you."

"A keeper," said King Andrew, rising up in his bed with a slow persistence determined by old age. "At this hour? What is a keeper doing here at this hour?"

"Please sire, Keeper Martin says it is a matter of utmost import."

The monarch stretched arms to full length and began his long, slow turn to put feet to floor, causing the chancellor to scramble for the royal slippers.

"Keeper Martin did you say?"

"Yes sire, Keeper Martin, head of all the Keepers of the Lore," said Yi, sighing with relief, as he just barely placed the slippers beneath his sire's feet as the king touched them to the hard floor.

"What is Keeper Martin doing here at this hour?" King Andrew cleared sleep from his eyes. "A king needs his sleep you know, especially at my age."

"I assure you sire, I wouldn't wake you unless it was a matter of import—which I am assured it is—though the keeper would not address the matter directly, sire. There is a look about him, as if he has just returned from a very long journey—a look of fatigue in the eyes, an unkempt beard. It is unlike Keeper Martin to have an unkempt beard.

"He wishes to speak to you alone. Rather mysterious, I must say. I will go talk to him if it is your wish, sire, and tell him to come back at a more appropriate time."

The king raised a hand to the chancellor's shoulder, using it to lift heavy bones from his plush bed. "There will be no need, Chancellor Yi. I am already roused. Tell him I will be along presently."

Father Tenuus shot a worried scowl to the chancellor as the two returned to the hall.

"I told you we should have waited a few more hours," he said in his lowest baritone voice. "Who is it that is here again, Keeper Q'yer or Keeper Martin, I always get the two mixed—"

"Come along, and lower your voice!"

38

"Oh, that's right, the Keeper Q'yer is that nice, younger man. Keeper Martin is distinguished and graying… His hair, that is… It must be Keeper Martin that has arrived."

"You're the one that's graying, and it's not your hair," said Chancellor Yi in a barely audible voice as he strode away down the hall. Father Tenuus had managed to annoy him as usual and he drowned the other's further comments by blowing his reddened nose a few dozen times into a long white handkerchief.

Further disturbed by the boisterous voices in the hall, the young princess had listened with great enthusiasm. Images of the troubled dream quickly fell away as she waited until the two old men passed by her door. A keeper here in the palace—and especially at this hour—was a sure sign of trouble. For an instant, she was almost sorry her wish had come true, but she quickly waved that off. Anything that brought a breath of life into Imtal Palace was more than welcome.

The balcony overlooking the entrance hall was not far from her chambers. After she pulled a robe loosely over her shoulders, she ran to it. A flood of thoughts exploded through her young mind and several expressions of glee escaped her anxious lips during the brief walk.

While she looked on, a still drowsy king greeted the great Lore Keeper. She chuckled a bit at her father's dowdy appearance in his night robe and slippers, and at the gauche waddle due to the slickness of the smooth floor. The special significance of the meeting struck—especially when private chambers were entered without Chancellor Yi . This was further compounded by the arrival of a second visitor shortly after the two had entered the chamber and closed the door.

To get a better view of the newcomer, Adrina had to slip from the shadows of the balcony, for his back already had been turned to her when she spotted him. The distinct robes of his office were an easy clue as to who the man was as he removed his riding cloak and wrapped it over his arm. Father Jacob was first minister to King Andrew, head of the priesthood, and there was no mistaking the great swirling circles of white that decorated the sleeves of his otherwise black robe.

A visit by both men, especially at this late hour, was unprecedented and in her mind Adrina found only one answer.

"War," she whispered in reverent tones. The Minors were at war.

***

"Your Highness, Princess Adrina?" called out a distant voice in her ear.

Grudgingly Adrina stirred.

Her room was still dark, the world still blurry. It couldn't have been day. She closed her eyes and attempted to return to sleep.

"Are you all right, princess?"

Adrina recognized the voice of the burly captain of the guard now. She felt his hands on her legs and screamed. The scream, a long and high-pitched wail, brought guards from down the hall and Lady Isador, and roused King Andrew from his bed.

"Get your hands off me! Go away!"

"I think you should come with me, princess," said Captain Brodst.

Again he attempted to help her up. Again she screamed.

Motherly Lady Isador came barreling toward the captain screaming, "Hurry, hurry!" to the guards that were right behind her.

"Get your hands off her. Guards, guards!" she continued.

Eyes wide, Adrina watched Lady Isador tangle with Captain Brodst.

From down the hall, she heard her father's moaning and the clamor of heavy feet running toward her. Suddenly she realized she was lying in the hallway beside the balcony. She slapped a hand to her mouth as the events of last night came flooding back to her—the voices in the hall, Keeper Martin and Father Jacob's unprecedented visit.

"By the Mother," Adrina whispered as she broke out in laughter. The scene *was* comical. Her lying in the hall. Small-statured Lady Isador barreling down on the burly captain. Her father waddling down the hall in his night slippers. Guards running to her rescue.

Lady Isador stopped wrestling with the captain and stared at Adrina.

"She's lost her mind." The governess gasped.

Lady Isador swept Adrina up in a motherly, smothering embrace.

"You oaf," she screamed at Captain Brodst, "what did you think you were doing?"

King Andrew stopped directly in front of Adrina and Isador, and then turned to stare at the captain. Uneasily four guardsmen were pointing their long spears at Captain Brodst. One of the guardsmen's hands was shaking so violently that the spear was swaying back and forth mightily.

Embarrassment replaced Adrina's cheer. She had no idea how she would diffuse the situation. She looked from the captain to the guards to King Andrew to Lady Isador. Apparently, no one else knew what to do either. The guards maintained their stance, spears pointing at their beloved captain. King Andrew scratched his head and attempted to wipe sleep from his tired eyes. Lady Isador was trying to hug the life out of her. Captain Brodst was staring down the four guardsmen, almost tempting them to charge.

Adrina let Lady Isador help her to her feet, and then she walked toward Captain Brodst and took his hand.

"Thank you," she said, "will you escort me to my chambers now?"

The captain walked her to her chambers, where Adrina thanked him again, then closed the door. For five days afterward no mention of the incident was made to her, though she did notice that any time Captain Brodst came near Lady Isador he became very defensive. When this happened, Adrina would hide a smile with her hand and usually Captain Brodst would turn away, an irritated look in his eye.

Adrina spent those days trying to piece together what had transpired behind closed chamber doors the night of the unexpected visit. That is, when Lady Isador or Chancellor Yi weren't giving her lessons on courtship and etiquette, and discounting the horrible day she spent with Rudden Klaiveson. The more she probed for answers, the more intrigued she became. No one in the whole of Imtal Palace would talk about the visit—Emel included.

She was working on a plan to change that. Emel would talk. She had only to find the right time and the right words.

***

Across a vast open courtyard, on the far side of the summer parade grounds, lay the palace stables. Performing his perfunctory duties as acting sergeant had delayed Emel and by the time he had arrived at the palace stables the others of his company had been and gone.

His steed, fittingly dubbed Ebony Lightning because it was jet black and could outpace even stallions bred for the king's swiftest messengers, still waited in its stall. He had known the appointed time of first formation and so he had not hurried—then he had still had a full half hour.

There was a reason Ebony Lightning was the swiftest steed in Imtal Proper and maybe even in all the land, and that was because of the special bond between horse and rider. Before and after every ride, Emel rubbed the horse down from the poll of its head to the dock of its tail, up and down each powerful leg. In his proud eyes Ebony was the tallest stallion in all the lands, and when Emel rode him it was from this height that he looked down upon the world.

Emel would have given anything to be like the Kingdom huntsmen, free like the four winds. His skills as a tracker stemmed from these desires. He had even pulled several short assignments at High Road Garrison—the last being during the past winter and spring—which allowed him to exercise these desires. He had not been able to take Ebony Lightning with him then, but now things were different—since the animal was from the king's stocks, and, while he had cared for the great steed for many years and been its only rider, it was only recently that he had been given the horse, a reward for services rendered.

He had been putting the finishing touches on the rubdown when the unexpected visitor had found him. Now he could only watch from afar as the other riders began to file through the outer palace gates and listen to the ridemaster's call, knowing the evident anger in the tone. A determined Princess Adrina had found him. From the expression in her eyes and the saddlebags beside her, Emel knew without doubt what she wanted, yet he maintained his plea one last time.

"Adrina, I will say this one more time, please give me back the harness and let me go. They're passing through the palace gates. Damn you and your foolishness."

Adrina batted thick eyelashes. "Emel, please, I want to go riding with you. I'll have my father talk to the ridemaster if need be."

"Adrina, it's not the ridemaster I'm worried about. Now let me go."

Adrina dangled the harness in front of him, the only harness that remained in the stables—as far as Emel knew. Adrina had carefully hidden the others.

"No, not until you say yes."

"I'm late and I am going to be in real trouble." Emel was clearly flustered.

"Just ask, my horse is already saddled, I won't complain or anything, I promise. I'll even be quiet. I won't say a word the entire way. You know how much I want to leave the palace… It's so dead, Emel, it's all dead… I see nothing but these damned gray walls and all I want to do is scream, shout at the top of my lungs and curse the whole of the world."

There was evident sadness in her words and Emel understood it. He understood what it was to be swallowed by the sense of loss, to mourn for so long that all you remembered was the sadness—forever retreating to that hollow place in the pit of your gut where sadness swells from—yet his oath was to the Kingdom and not to her.

Also, he had sudden visions of spending another winter and spring at High Road Garrison.

"I never hit a girl before, but if I have to, I will," said Emel.

"I am not a girl, I am a woman, and I… if you hit me—" The princess paused. Still determined, she continued with a cool tone that was almost callous, "If you hit me, I'll hit you back."

Emel believed her. She had been trained in hand-to-hand combat the same as he had—an actuality that Adrina was proud of—and the fact that she had bested him once or twice on the competition field led him to believe that she could be capable of it again.

"Okay, you win, I'll ask. Now let's hurry," said Emel, hoping to snatch the harness from relaxed hands, and that is just what he did. He put the harness in place and was in the saddle nearly as fast as the wind—by his standards—but, by the time that he had finished, the persistent princess was mounted and cleverly awaiting him just beyond the stable in the parade grounds.

"Adrina, please, just forget it."

"I've never been on an adventure. I'm all set for excitement," answered Adrina, pleading her case with the tone of her voice, still holding to the melodramatic.

"We aren't actually leaving until tomorrow. Today was to be practice. There are a dozen other guardsmen who will willingly take my position. Please just leave me alone. I have to show the ridemaster I know what I am doing. Besides, the ride to Alderan City on the edge of West Deep is hardly an adventure. I'll be back in a few weeks. I'll take you riding then."

"I don't care, I just want to be away, as far away from Imtal as possible. Besides, I know something of the reason we are going to Alderan by the sea."

Adrina directed her eyes at him—it was mostly true.

"*We* aren't going. I am going. If I don't hurry, I'll miss my chance too. Ridemaster Gabrylle is sure to be angry."

Adrina knew the departure was shrouded in secrecy. Ridemaster Gabrylle had been told to make the journey look like training for the young palace ridesmen. Adrina had heard this from a kitchen cook that bedded the ridemaster. She owed the rather large woman a string of favors for the telling.

"Seven days ago, my father had two important visitors in the night. One was Keeper Martin, head of all Lore Keepers. The other, Father Jacob, first minister, head of the priesthood. Keeper Martin brought grave news from the Far South."

"Really?" asked Emel, "You're not jesting are you?"

"Do I look like I am? By the Mother, I tell you it is the truth. You didn't know this, did you?"

The thought of lying outright crossed Emel's mind, but the truth was that he didn't know. As far as he knew no one had been told of this, though he was admittedly extremely curious.

"No," he said truthfully, definitively.

"I heard the whole plan," said Adrina. She was lying and vowed to repent later, if it worked.

"How do you know? I wasn't even told, and I am a Sergeant at Arms." He made the title sound lofty.

"And I am the king's daughter, aren't I? I am privileged to certain information that you aren't."

Emel was taken aback by her words, but believed her. Possibly she really did know, he thought.

"All right, but you have to tell me everything you know. Deal?"

"Of course, first you must tell me the reason we travel to Alderan. Then if you tell me the truth, I will tell you what I know."

"We travel to Alderan to meet a ship that sailed from Wellison in the South three days ago."

"Thank you."

Adrina spurred her mount on.

The two moved across the pristine green of the open parade grounds at a slow trot. Emel purposefully reined his mount in despite its urge to race away and chase the wind. He wanted to find out what Adrina knew, for then he could ride off, leaving her behind without a care—or so he hoped.

"Well. Aren't you going to tell me something?" asked Emel.

Adrina wasn't about to fall for this ploy. "Yes, I'm going to tell you, just not right now. Only if you talk to the ridemaster. Is it a deal?"

Flustered and confident he'd never find out what Adrina knew, also sure she would chase him down even if he charged his mount out the gates, Emel waived his better judgment. He agreed to her wishes. Anyway, he knew the final words of approval were not his. Maybe if King Andrew said a final no, Adrina would tell him what she knew anyway—if he stayed on her good side.

"Deal," Emel said, "I'll talk to the ridemaster."

Chapters 3 and 4: Review Questions

1. Why does Lady Isador tell Princess Adrina "Down, down, down dear. No wonder that hem looked all wrong. Mustn't stand on tiptoes."?
___
___

2. Seth feels helpless as he waits in the antechamber. He considers eavesdropping. Do you think he should have? Would you have eavesdropped if you were Seth?
___
___
___

3. Why are Vilmos' parents so frightened when he tells what happened with the bear?
___
___
___

4. Why does Brother Liyan think Seth is afraid of leaving?
___
___

5. Why do you think Emel calls Adrina a "fair-weather friend"?
___
___

6. Why does Chancellor Yi wake up King Andrew in the middle of the night?
___
___
___

7. Did Captain Brodst really attack Adrina or was it a misunderstanding? Summarize what happened and why.
___
___
___

8. What does Adrina take from Emel that prevents him from doing his duties, and why?
___
___
___

9. Why do you think Emel's horse is called Ebony Lightning, and why do you think the king gave the horse to him?
___
___
___

Words to Watch

Complacent	Lingering	Charismatic
Perpetually	Mocking	Remorse
Relinquish	Pensive	Enchantment
Sermon	Methodical	Rebuke
Intervene	Perfunctory	Crescendo
Impart	Consciously	Dissipate
Wisdom	Sinister	Sepulchral
Commitment	Bewildered	

Chapter Five: Realization

The hours passed slowly in the peaceful hollow Vilmos had retreated to, its gentle serenity carefully lulling him into mindless complacency. Thoughts of returning home seemed so distant, so very distant. After all, he could dwell in the valley forever, couldn't he?

There was a finality in the thoughts that frightened him, and it was only this that ended his feelings of complacency and propelled the urge to return home to the foremost thought in his mind. With one last look down over *his* valley, Vilmos turned and walked away, leaving the peaceful vale far behind in a few powerful strides.

Strange though it seemed, the return trek was never as easy as the initial folding of thoughts one on top of the other that it took to get to the peaceful vale. No, the trek home was a long and arduous journey through a darkened land. Vilmos had to pass along the little country path that parted the dark wood and run for some distance veiled from the sun, with a perpetually icy wind at his back. He had to cross the distance from the woods to the village.

The next step of the journey was to enter the quaint country home that was his father's. His face set in a heavy mask of personal anguish, he did so on his tiptoes, moving slowly and quietly. He crossed to his room and closed the door without a sound. Approaching the bed, *his* bed, he sat down unaware of the gaunt, still figure already present. A moment for adjustment taken, Vilmos opened his eyes and retreated from his special place—the place he could have retreated back to with a simple folding of thoughts but which never relinquished him without first warning him that the world was a cruel and callous place.

That he would remain in his room throughout the rest of the morning was already a given. He found contentment by idly sitting on the edge of his bed where he could gaze out the clear open window and think of nothing in particular. And when he finally did venture out of his room, it was not until the midday had come and passed.

Upon cursory inspection, Vilmos discovered his father had already departed. On Seventhday, which was today, his father met with the Three Village Assembly. He was sure they would discuss the recent bear attack. Goose bumps ran up and down his back. He could have ended up just like the girl from Olex Village—and only Lillath would've cared.

A cherished notion to run away vaulted from his mind. There was work that needed to be done. Helping his mother, Lillath, brought Vilmos happiness, even though he considered "housework" a woman's chore.

Whistling a little tune, quaint and cheerful, he diligently started. Sweeping the floors was an easy task, so he tackled that first. He swept out the kitchen and the long, oblong floor of the visiting room in a matter of minutes. Bedrooms and halls were next and after them, as always, the porch. He was sweating now and the cool perspiration felt good. It was "honest work" he did, or so his mother said.

He paused for a time, though not long. Wood blocks still needed to be split and piled by the wood shed. His room needed to be cleaned. The bed made. His few belongings gathered and placed back into the wooden chest that lay at the foot of his bed.

After several hours of continuous labor and an examination by his mother, Vilmos was finished. Joyfully, he scrambled into the kitchen to sneak something to eat, yet as always it was his ill-fated luck to be caught.

"Vil-MOS! What are you doing?" Lillath asked. She tried to hide laughter with her hand. "Never cease eating do you?"

"But I am hungry."

"Go ahead. Don't eat too much. We'll have an early dinner. Don't forget today is Seventhday and we'll all go to the service, won't we?"

Vilmos frowned, then replied, "Yes, mother," but in his mind, he wished they would not go. He hated the long sermons, during which he often fell asleep, which got him into even more trouble.

In a moment Vilmos knew that without fail he would be told to review the history and as he didn't want to do that, he gathered up his bread and cheese and tried to leave.

"Not so fast. Hold on a minute Vilmos," Lillath said, "forgetting something?"

"No mother. I put the bread back into the box, honest."

In a blur he was out the door and headed toward his room, sanctuary one solitary step away when the voice reached him.

"Mustn't forget to study your history.

Someday you'll fill your father's position. Even with your faults." She added the last part in jest, but Vilmos didn't catch the false sarcasm in her voice immediately.

"And what faults are those?"

Lillath tried to hide her smile with a shielding hand. "I'm only joking. Go study the Book."

Vilmos lifted the heavy book from its resting place. Usually the Great Book would lie before him the remainder of the day, but mostly his mind would wander. Vilmos turned back to his mother and asked, "Mother, are there other books? I mean, surely all knowledge cannot be contained in one book."

"Don't ever let your father hear you talk like that." Lillath paused and stared at the boy. Her tone became milder. "Books are a rare, rare thing in the land. It takes years, lifetimes, to pen a single tome. And only a true book smith can press scrolls into such a leather binding as befits the Great Book."

Vilmos smiled. He opened the book about midway, and then set it down. Normally he would have turned away immediately and stared out the window. But today the book seemed to want to open to a particular pair of pages, a group of pages shuffled and he was staring at a new section of the book. Thinking fondly of what his mother had said, he mumbled his way through the inscribed words.

With the simple lives of children, the story began...

Thousands of years ago wars ravaged the lands, spread by the slow incursion of the race called Man to the brother races until it seemed that humankind would not endure.

Great-Father had not intervened until this time, he had spread his gifts thinly out to each of the brother races, imparting each with but one simple gift, but even the wise and the great could not have foretold the coming of the scourge of evil spread by a maligning of those same simple gifts...

Time eternal evolves in great circles and the All-Father knew and understood this only too well. So as the evil scourge was finally defeated and the First Age came to an end, he planned carefully for the future by selecting and gathering a few of those last children and imparting upon them greater knowledge and wisdom than most. Some he taught how to outwit time itself. Some he conditioned as watch-wardens to look for the signs of the next Coming, the next Age of humankind. Others he cast into the never-ending circle of time itself so that their spiritual forms could wind their way through its realm. These were the lost children and he appointed a single guardian over them all…

To balance it all, there was one who was both good and evil, fated by destiny to become part of time itself…

Vilmos frowned and stopped reading. He'd thought he had read, or had had read to him, every page of the Great Book at one time or another, but he had never read this page. It puzzled him, and he reread it. What did it all mean? What was the lesson?

Confused, he closed the book and stared at its cover. Later he opened it to a different section.

***

Vilmos' father did not come home until late that evening. Vil had been delayed in a special advisory session. Apparently a series of bear attacks had taken place in Two Falls Village a day's ride to the north, and huntsmen and trackers from the surrounding villages were preparing to track down the great black bear. There would be no one allowed to travel outside the village until the bear was caught.

Vilmos, who had been listening intently at the door to his room, suddenly found he had an entire evening to do as he pleased—that is as long as he didn't venture into his father's eyesight. He thought Great-Father was truly smiling down upon him.

"What luck!" exclaimed Vilmos as he jumped onto his bed. "What to do? What to do?"

With final commitment, he closed his eyes and retreated to his special place. The vale was a beautiful place toward evening with a red-pink haze held in the darkening sky spreading outward into the heavens in striking hues of orange and red. The hunter eagle was gone from the sky now so Vilmos contented himself by sitting on the very brink of the high cliff he had chosen. Occasionally he would throw a rock up in the air, catch it midair and then let it lazily float down to the ground like a feather.

Suddenly tired, he yawned. His vision began to fade out as slumber entered his thoughts and within minutes he fell asleep. Lulled by his fatigue, he was caught in the quasi-world he had created. Sleep for him was always accompanied by dreams, although unlike others who often forgot their dreams upon waking, Vilmos remembered his.

The dream began. It was a strange and frightening dream, the only dream that had played out before him the whole of his life as far back as he could remember.

The words of the Great Book that had lain before him most of the day came to mind, corrupted by the evil of the dream…

The creature of darkness descended to the earth from the heavens, wreaking havoc across the land's face, once more reclaiming that which was his, that which was denied to him.

Look weak creatures! Look what you have let loose! Look what you have freed to provide for your demise! I am what you most fear! I am He. A name cursed for all eternity. I possess the forbidden name, never spoken lest it invoke the greatest of all evil. I am that evil. I can speak its name. Do you know what that evil is? What does humankind fear so very much?

You fear yourself. You fear that which humankind was, and still is. You fear the darkness of your soul…

The boy, who was Vilmos as he looked in

upon his dream as if from a distance, saw the evil one and looked into his eyes. The darkness within was well known to him. Its origin of rebirth was known. Held entranced by its call, he moved his hand forward to help it but was stopped by a sharp, stifling pain that shot through him. The shock and ache made his small body writhe as it carried him away.

Unconsciousness befell him, yet the images and the agony were still clear in his thoughts when he awoke some hours later crying out into the darkness, huddled in a cold, sweated corner, his body clenched and trembling.

"No!! No!! It will not be!" screamed Vilmos, perspiration dripped off his forehead.

"No, no, no," he continued through the sobs, unable to block out the lingering picture of the shadows in his mind, especially the evil, mocking grimace that laughed a deep, hideous laugh and the cold jet-black eyes that seemed to haunt every corner of his mind.

This was the worst dream he could recall. For a time the dreams had stopped completely, then they had returned with renewed fervor. Each night the vision came. Repeatedly it played, relentless. Each time growing worse, because each time it became more realistic. Now it was as if the Dark One was in the very room Vilmos occupied.

Normally he would have simply escaped to his private point to stare out across the vast expanse below, feeling more at home and at peace there than he had ever felt in his own home. However, this night Vilmos did not want to return there. Something was wrong, though what, he didn't know. Content to remain in his room in the dark, staring into nothingness, desperately trying to remember something that he knew was important, his mind raced in a million different directions.

Throughout the night he lay gazing into the darkness, searching for something that appeared to be just beyond his grasp. His concentration was so great that he had not moved in the entire time and when the sun rose bright and beautiful into a clear sky, he did not enjoy its beauty. His mood only turned from pensive to dreary. The new day brought him only misery, as he knew it would. His body, stiff and sluggish, moving with the aches and pains of one well beyond his years, did not respond well to his desires and again it was a long, slow process to coax stiff muscles into movement.

After eating breakfast and methodically performing his perfunctory chores, his thoughts filled with dread. The tutor would come this day. Weary and fatigued, Vilmos trudged back to his room, slumped onto the bed, all his energy spent. Utter exhaustion played out on his face, though he didn't understand why.

The instant eyes closed, consciously or unconsciously, he drifted away to his special place. It had been calling to him in the back of his mind all that morning.

***

A chilling breeze blew through the vale. A wind that had never before been cold. Today something felt different, as if he were not alone. Worriedly, he scanned the little vale, its steep slopes and its large open floor. He was indeed alone or so he hoped.

He became a great silver eagle, fearless and swift. The dive from his favored cliff was accomplished in one powerful leap. Wings sliced the air and made it sing. Down into the vale's depths the eagle swept, with great speed and agility. The silver eagle's keen eyes had instantly spotted its prey and now it raced toward the unsuspecting valley hare.

This was the intruder in his domain, thought Vilmos. He would crush the life from his prey and then would indeed be alone.

He swept up the valley hare in razor sharp talons. The warm and fleshy hare writhed pitifully and cried out for escape. The eagle did not heed its cry, but a part of Vilmos did and he forced the great eagle to release the hare.

"Do you know what it is that you are doing?" beckoned a voice into his mind.

Vilmos was startled.

"N-no," he replied warily. The voice was somehow familiar.

Momentarily the vision of the eagle faltered. For an instant Vilmos stood on the high, raised cliff staring into the cold northerly wind. Then he was propelled back into the razor-taloned, silver eagle.

"It is called non-corporeal stasis, an out of body experience," said the other with evident wisdom.

"What are you saying? What does that mean? Are you here to take me away?"

Vilmos ceased being the eagle altogether, yet the cliff was not the place he returned to. Instead, he stood in the middle of the valley and searched in all directions for the source of the mysterious voice.

"*Look*. Look about you. What do you see?" commanded the voice.

Vilmos did as bid.

"I see the valley and nothing else."

"Yes that is correct, now look beyond the valley. Extend your thoughts and open your mind. Now what do you see?" The voice flowed with warmth and again Vilmos sensed a familiarity in it.

"I see only the valley," Vilmos replied.

"No," said the other with vehemence, "*Look, look again*. Search beyond the valley. What do you see?"

Vilmos didn't like this game and clenched his fists in anger. "I see nothing."

"*Open* the window to your soul. You *will* see. *Look*." said the presence.

Compelled to do as told Vilmos looked inside himself. He saw the door to his soul and he opened it. Beyond, in the shadows, he saw himself, lying in his bed, in his father's house.

"What do you see?" the other asked.

"N-nothing!"

"*What do you see?*" commanded the voice.

"I see myself, I see myself!" Vilmos paused. His voice filled with surprise as he continued, "but how, I don't understand?"

"That is what the experience is. Your body remains on the physical plane and your spirit searches beyond. You were truly flying. You really were the lone eagle flying over a valley of your own creation." The ominous voice seemed to close in on Vilmos. "You are a master of non-corporeal stasis, yet do not forget that all things have mirrors on the physical plane."

"How is this possible?" the skeptic in Vilmos inquired.

"Think, before you speak. *Look within, you know it is possible*." The tone of the voice became sinister. "As is everything."

"I am afraid. I want to go home—I want to go home now."

"But Vilmos you are home. *This is your home*. This is the sanctuary you alone created," the voice rang with heavy truths.

"No, I want to go home," insisted Vilmos, "I am afraid."

"Well you should be Vilmos, you should be very afraid." Vilmos pictured black eyes drawing up before him. "This experience leaves your physical self completely without defense. It is open to attack from any force or forces that wish to enter it. Any spirit can enter your body while your own spirit travels. And there it can grow and thrive!"

Vilmos jumped back, his face drawn and pale

with shock. Bewildered eyes looked out. His body shivered beyond control. Everything within him told him to run away, to hide, though he could not. It was then that he recognized the voice, though vaguely. It was then his panic grew to despair and he feared for his very soul.

"It is you! This is what I was trying to remember."

"Yes it is," said the voice with mocking overtones.

***

Gripped with fear, Vilmos stood unable to move. He looked out over the valley that had once seemed peaceful, only now regaining the point as he fought to focus his mind. He felt alone, very alone, though he knew he wasn't. He cocked his head, left and right, forward and back, searching. But his search was in vain because he truly was alone. There was no one else with him.

Waiting to hear the voice again and ensure he wasn't just daydreaming, Vilmos remained absolutely still. Only his own gasping breaths broke the silence, nothing more.

"Where are you? Show yourself," Vilmos called out. The only answer Vilmos received was the sound of wind rushing over the point and the returning echoes of his voice as it faded away and blended into the wind.

The vale was empty; the ridge, empty.

"Looking for me?" came a voice from behind him.

Startled, Vilmos jumped. His heart pumped faster and faster. Breathing became taxing. It seemed he could not grasp any air. He spun around, faltering and falling to the hard, rocky surface of the vantage point. He pulled himself to his feet, and shook defiant fists in the air.

"I will not hurt you," said the now charismatic voice from behind him.

Vilmos spun around again. "Where are you? Show yourself."

"I am here."

"But how? A moment ago, I was alone," said Vilmos as he turned to look in the direction of the voice.

"A moment ago, I was not here," said the venerable man who now stood in plain view in front of Vilmos. He was by far the oldest man Vilmos had ever seen. His appearance was one of such frailty and weakness that Vilmos imagined a heavy wind lifting him from his feet and casting him about in the air like a feather.

The aged man leaned his weight against his long, misshaped, walking stick, edging poised lips closer to Vilmos' ear. "Do not let the body fool you boy," he whispered, "I will not *blow* away in the wind."

Just then a cold, harsh wind started to rip across the point. With each passing second, it increased in force until it was a gale of great strength. Very soon, Vilmos found he could no longer stand in its face. He crouched to his knees and then to his belly. The old man did not so much as twitch.

"Please stop it!" screamed Vilmos.

"I cannot. Only you may stop it."

Not wanting to fall from the ledge to his death, Vilmos huddled close to the ground trying to maintain his grip with desperate fingers. "I don't know how to stop it. Let me go. I want to go."

"Then surely you shall perish." The man spoke sternly, his voice lacking any hint of remorse.

Vilmos trembled. "Do you mean die?"

"As surely as you were born."

Truth in the other's words stung Vilmos, similar to the dirt in his eyes. He knew without a doubt that he would indeed perish if he failed to stop the wind.

Wind whipped at him. Dust stung his face and blew into his eyes. And while Vilmos could barely see through this dust and dirt, he felt he had to see the old one again. Gazing through stinging dirt proved a difficult task accomplished only with shielding hands. To Vilmos' dismay, the man stood straight and tall, tall as the twisted staff he carried. He faced the wind and his stance still did not vary.

Suddenly the man did not appear so aged to Vilmos. In fact, somehow he seemed different, as if Vilmos saw another standing there in the old man's place. "I do not deny that you have powers beyond my grasp," began Vilmos, "but I don't understand the point of the test. I don't know what to do."

"Vilmos, *use* that which you already know. *Use the skills you possess. Use them now!*" The man spoke powerfully.

Compelled by the enchantment of the voice, Vilmos made a vigorous attempt. He concentrated, trying to make the wind stop. He clasped his eyes tightly together, held his breath, clenched his fists so firmly that his fingernails dug into his palms. The wind did not desist; it continued to lash at him with increased vigor.

Fearing for his very life, Vilmos tried again. He thought about the wind and wanting to stop it. In rebuke, the blast of the wind started to push him toward the edge of the cliff. Vilmos dug his fingers into the dirt trying desperately to hold on, grasping and clawing until his hands were bloody, but to no avail.

His fingers pulsated with pain. Vilmos screamed and pleaded desperately for assistance. He turned his head wildly back and forth, wary of the approaching drop. "I don't want to die… please help me… how can you just stand there, help me! Please, I beg you."

"*Reach inside yourself for the power*. It is there. The power lives within you. You have used it many times before, though you didn't know why or exactly how. *You are the power Vilmos*. It yearns to be released from within you. *Release it.*"

"Please help me." Vilmos sounded pathetic. "P-please."

"Release the power Vilmos," repeated the other, "let it go. I am giving you a reason to use your power. I give you your life! *Do it now, quickly, or you will DIE!*"

The voice was commanding again, Vilmos felt compelled to do as invoked. He had to prove he could stop the wind. Somewhere within was the key, a key that must be found. It had been so much easier before. He had never really tried to use the power. Previously it had just come to him when he needed it. He needed it now, and it wouldn't come.

"Hurry, Vilmos. You must hurry!" spoke the man with a hint of anxiety in his voice.

In time, Vilmos found the object of his inward search. The strength was there.

Still unsure exactly how he was supposed to make the wind stop, Vilmos decided to let his mind drift. His thoughts wandered until he found a helpful clue. As he anticipated, the solution to his dilemma seemed to seep into his mind.

It had always been there.

"Quickly, Vilmos!" The man spoke frantically. "*You must release the power now.*"

A test of the power within forced the wind to flicker. Strength flowed to Vilmos unbidden. He bathed in its caress; it felt so wonderful.

Magic isn't evil; it is beautiful.

Vilmos knew what he had to do to make the wind cease. Now he would do it.

The man screamed, "Vil-mos, release the power, release it now before it is too late." His anxiety increased with each passing second. "Hurry Vilmos. You must release the power now.

Let it go, feel it flow."

Vilmos perceived a peculiar scratching at the back of his mind, something loomed closer. Magic isn't evil, he reminded himself, the words flowing to him again.

"Go on try it," whispered the voice, "set it free."

Vilmos shook his head to rid himself of the irritating scratching.

"I will, I will," Vilmos said.

For an instant, Vilmos toyed with the wind. The gale stopped full, then started again with sudden vigor. Vilmos shook his head again to rid himself of the irritating scratching at the back of his mind.

Was it a whisper?

Seemingly as if simply acknowledging the whisper existed was enough, the voice came again. "No Vilmos," it whispered.

Vilmos shook his head again, his concentration faltering. Irritated, the old man grabbed Vilmos about the shoulders and lifted him from the ground, shaking him violently.

"Do as you were told boy!" he screamed, his razor sharp finger nails pushing into Vilmos' arms.

With untold power captivated in a crisp, clear voice, the newcomer spoke again. "It is a trick Vilmos. Look closely, see his true form. Evil comes in many shadings, but you can always see through it if your vision is clear and your mind is centered. Search its form. *LOOK!*"

The wind stopped dead; the old man released his grip. Vilmos fell to his knees.

"No Vilmos, it is not true. Release the power. Do not listen to foul lies. *Release it now.*"

Heeding the will of the voice, the power of magic within Vilmos soared. Torn between the two choices, unsure which to follow, who spoke the truth, or what to do, Vilmos clasped his hands to his head. His mind reeled with pain. He wanted to curl up into a ball and disappear.

Unchecked the power within grew to a crescendo, reaching beyond Vilmos' control. His wild eyes stared in disbelief as crazed thoughts continued to spin through his mind. He was the power, the master of all he surveyed; he would release the force within.

"Vilmos, in the name of Great-Father, I command you *AWAKEN!*" spoke a third voice with overwhelming sincerity and vast fear. In the haze of Vilmos' consciousness, the voice was a distant untouchable shadow. The power within was so inviting and warm, he did not want to let it go.

The old one grew greedy and smiled an evil grimace. "YES, Vilmos, can you feel it? Yes. That's a good boy. Now, *USE* it."

Vilmos discerned and separated the perceived voices. The newest, the faint, distant one overridden with fear and heart wrenching pain, was feminine. The crisp, clear voice of the newcomer was calm and compelling. The voice of the old one demanded action.

"Are you the evil one?" Vilmos asked.

The instant disbelief entered his mind, the enchantment was lost. The energy within him dissipated. Vilmos looked dead into the old man's eyes and understood the guise.

"You truly are the evil one," said an amazed Vilmos. As he spoke, both strangers disappeared. The words reverberated in his thoughts.

With the releasing of the deadlocked gaze on the wall opposite his bed, the vision ended. Complete and utter confusion played across Vilmos' face. The sepulchral dream had ended, though its images were still held in his mind's eye. It had seemed so real, but how could it have been? He had never left his room; he would not have perished. It was only another daydream, a dreadful one.

He reflected upon what he had seen there and was deathly afraid, for normally when the dream ended the evil of the Dark One disappeared. This time the dream was different, Vilmos could recall shapes and images, even the form the evil one had taken.

It no longer seemed that the evil one was just part of a dream. He remembered the raging winds and the fear. It was then that an alarm of distress sounded within. Again there was a small part that he just couldn't remember—he had seen something, but what was it?

The images became steadily less clear as he strained to focus on them. Pain in his hands caused all thoughts to drift away and when he looked down at them, opening and closing them with evident agony, he knew the pain had been real.

Physically and mentally drained of all its energy, his body was an empty shell with all its stamina gone. Vilmos wanted to sleep, yet he dared not close his eyes. The dream had been real, not imagined, he reminded himself.

Aghast, he curled up in the corner, fitting his small form into a tightly curled ball. The pain had been real, the dream been real, his mind repeated relentlessly.

Chapter 5: Word Jumble

Complacent	Lingering	Bewildered
Perpetually	Mocking	Charismatic
Relinquish	Pensive	Remorse
Sermon	Methodical	Enchantment
Intervene	Perfunctory	Rebuke
Impart	Consciously	Crescendo
Wisdom	Lingering	Dissipate
Commitment	Sinister	Sepulchral

Word jumble: Unjumble the letters of these vocabulary words. Hint: Column 1.

Pritma
Lcntcoaemp
Dosimw
Moresn
Teplyperlua
Squlinreih
Tvneeerin
Mtentoimmc

Word jumble: Unjumble the letters of these vocabulary words. Hint: Column 2.

Ucsoioncyls
Greininlg
Htdicleoma
Kcmogni
Vneisep
Cfptenuroyr
Trsiines

Word jumble: Unjumble the letters of these vocabulary words. Hint: Column 3.

Ocsnderec
Wdrdeeebli
Psisditae
Tantnemhcen
Mtcasirharc
Rmseero
Ebkuer
Lhrasepluc

Words to Watch

Errant	Recruit	Clamber
Inevitable	Sergeant	Appearance
Pittance	Congratulate	Serenity
Gallant	Betrothal	Ponderous
Invasion	Wayward	Spectacle
Consequence	Diminish	Spectacular
Unbearable	Cobbled	

Chapter Six: Permission

A strong wind out of the northwest blew long strands of dark hair into Adrina's eyes. Every now and again as she looked down into High King's Square, she tucked the errant strands behind her ear. Sunset was near, and the square was bustling with activity. Merchants packing their wares onto pack animals, townsfolk haggling for last minute deals and the inevitable array of jugglers, musicians, fire-eaters and the like trying to earn a pittance for their supper.

Adrina disliked the busyness in the square; nevertheless, she stared down into it. She was waiting for Emel to return with news from Ridemaster Gabrylle and the square afforded the best vantage point to witness the return of the horsemen. She was worried. Emel should have returned to the palace an hour ago—at least that is when he had told her he would return when she had parted with him at the palace gates.

Briefly, Adrina cast uneasy eyes westward. The sun was already beginning to dip below the horizon, soon it would be dark. Just then she noticed the northerly wind and a smile crossed her lips.

"Change comes," Adrina whispered.

As she turned back to stare down into the square, a distant sound came to her ears. It could be the clatter of hooves on cobbled stones.

She heard the sound again, though this time it seemed even more distant. Then trumpeters in the palace gate towers and at the city walls sounded off in response to the distant call and Adrina knew the far off call had to be that of a trumpet. Her eyes set with worry, she stared westward. Someone in the foothills, beyond the green fields that stretched out of view, was in trouble.

Trumpeters at the city walls sounded again—a cavalry call. Adrina knew the calls well—Emel had taught them to her—there was no mistaking the distinct call to arms. Imtal garrison riders would soon respond to the trumpeters' summons. Adrina's face flushed white. Emel was out there somewhere with Ridemaster Gabrylle and a group of unproven young guardsmen.

Her heart pounded in her ears, another call came from the city walls. A mounted guard was passing through the gates. Somewhere in the foothills a battle was surely taking place. Adrina had sudden grand visions of a full-scale invasion by the Bandit King of the North. Emel gallantly defending land and king. And the king's cavalry charging into the fray.

She held her breath until the call ended, realizing only as the call to arms faded into the wind the true consequences of such a thing. "Please Great-Father not Emel. He may be brash at times, but he is brave and true as any. The truth is, I would miss him dearly."

The silence that followed became unbearable

and Adrina retreated to her room. For a long time, she stared out her window. The dusk sky slowly darkened and night arrived. The trumpeters made no further calls and Adrina eventually let sleep take her.

***

Unsure what had awoken her, Adrina stirred. She dipped her hands into the basin beside her bed and eased sleep from her eyes with the cool water. High overhead the light of a full moon was filtering in through her window, casting long shadows about the room.

An attendant was replacing the coals in her fireplace. "Sorry Your Highness," she whispered. "I shouldn't have let the fire go out, but I wished not to disturb you. It looks to be a cold night and I was concerned."

"Yes," said Adrina, "summer is surely at an end."

The attendant finished her work and as she departed she said, "Good night, Your Highness."

Adrina nodded. She was watching the flames in the hearth slowly build.

Soon a low but cheerful fire began to fill her chamber with warmth. As Adrina bent down to put on her slippers, she noticed she was still dressed in her riding clothes. She changed into her nightclothes. Thankful Lady Isador hadn't found her sleeping thus. She would never have heard the end of it. She could hear the old governess now, "Proper ladies do not sleep in their day clothes."

A soft knock on the door followed by whispers caused her momentary alarm. "Lady Isador?"

"Do I sound like Lady Isador?" replied a voice in a hushed tone.

"Emel?" asked Adrina.

"Of course Emel. Are you going to let me in?"

"Just a minute." Adrina slipped a robe around her then opened the door. "Hurry up, hurry up. No one saw you come up here did they?"

"Do I look stupid? Close the door, close the door."

Adrina closed the door. She almost ran into his arms, but caught herself on the first step. "Must remember your station, dear," she whispered to herself—Lady Isador's words.

"You're muttering, I can't understand you. I nearly ran into that attendant of yours. I told her I was making my rounds. She seemed to believe me. I think she rather likes me. She is pretty don't you think?"

Noticing how handsome Emel looked in the pale light, Adrina stared—here before her was twice the man the son of Klaive was.

Their eyes met, she averted her eyes from his. "I was worried. I heard the trumpet calls and when you didn't return I thought something dreadful had happened to you."

Emel chuckled. "Something did happen and you're not going to believe me."

Adrina directed her eyes at Emel. Okay tell me, they said.

Emel started laughing again. "You wouldn't believe what happened to Ridemaster Gabrylle."

Go on, Adrina's eyes said.

"We were skirting the Braddabaggon foothills on the return. Twelve new recruits, never been on a mount before in their lives. Twelve more that'd done border patrol once or twice, but still rather new to riding. Three others, acting sergeants like me. Ridemaster Gabrylle had been cursing all day long. And out pops this lowland cat. The thing was seven feet long head to tail, all claws and teeth.

"It let out a cry and up went Ridemaster Gabrylle's bay. Ridemaster Gabrylle fell clear from his saddle and there he sat. One more hiss out of that cat sent the new recruits running scared. And they didn't just go in one direction. They all went in different directions. Half were clinging to their frightened mounts' necks and the other half were just trying to stay in the saddle.

"Ridemaster Gabrylle started screaming and cursing—it was then we noticed he'd broken his leg in the fall. He was spitting fire and those new recruits heard it and they panicked even more. They thought the cat was devouring poor Ridemaster Gabrylle. I didn't know whether to laugh, cry or help the ridemaster. It was comical as you please."

Adrina was laughing heartily now. She motioned to Emel to sit and hesitantly he joined her on the bed. He sat on one side, she on the other.

"Tell me the truth of it," Adrina said, "you ran too didn't you?"

"I did think about it. I didn't want to be there when Ridemaster Gabrylle got back into the saddle."

"What of the trumpets?" asked Adrina, tucking her long black hair back to one side.

"Oh that is even better." Emel paused and took a deep breath, his eyes following Adrina's hands. "Ridemaster Gabrylle's leg is broken and he demands that one of us snap the bone back into place. I'd never done it before and neither had anyone else. Gabrylle pointed at me and screamed, 'Brace the damn leg boy, I'll do it myself!' I gritted my teeth, closed my eyes and did it. Then I hear this snap, snap, SNAP!

"Gabrylle lets out this scream that chilled my bones and then we hear this trumpet call from Braddabaggon way. Gabrylle points at me and three others, 'Get that idiot boy back here,' he screams. We mounted. Then the call comes again. By that time, the city trumpeters are already responding and it's too late to do anything about stopping the garrison riders—you can't countermand a call to arms.

"We ride into the Braddabaggon a ways and at the bottom of this long round, we find this boy, sword in one hand, trumpeter's horn in the other. His mount gone and half crazed hearing Gabrylle's screams, he wouldn't let anyone near him. Finally the four of us get the sword away from him—by force—and we were returning when we see two entire columns of riders approaching lances, battle armor, shields. They were ready for a fight. Gabrylle buried his face in his hands and wept.

"Well actually, I thought he was weeping. Turns out he was trying so hard to hold in the laughter he was crying, broke leg and all."

"What happened next?" asked Adrina. She moved a little closer to Emel. "What happened to Ridemaster Gabrylle?"

"Oh he's all right, no riding for a couple months."

"No riding for a couple months," Adrina sounded disappointed as she suddenly realized that no ridemaster probably meant the end of their hopes for the trek to Alderan. "What of the journey to Alderan? Did they select the twelve guardsmen?"

"It would seem that the matter is more pressing than the ridemaster's injury." Emel paused, Adrina again moved closer to him. "I think we'll still mount and ride tomorrow."

"Think or know?" demanded Adrina, moving back.

"Well, I was told to rise before dawn and have my bags shouldered when I go to morning meal."

"So you made it, you're one of the twelve. Congratulations!"

"Wasn't much of a choice after the cat. But I won't be riding as a guardsman, Ridemaster Gabrylle says I'm to continue my apprenticeship into the rank of sergeant."

Adrina was glad of her friend's good fortune, still, disappointment played on her face. "I guess you never got the chance to ask the ridemaster about me, did you?"

"In all the excitement? No, I never got the chance. Still it seems the company will be much larger than expected. During the day something happened that I wasn't privy to. I don't know what it was but it's sure to be the reason why two full columns answered that alarm call.

"Seems Ridemaster Gabrylle wouldn't have lead the party anyway. Captain Brodst, my father, will. He's been elevated to King's Captain for the task. There'll be at least three garrison captains to boot. Seems half the city garrison is being roused and sent to the South. I don't know what's happened, but remember those two distinguished visitors in the night?"

Adrina nodded her head.

"The word is they'll be accompanying us."

***

Adrina greeted the new day with bleary eyes. After Emel had left she hadn't slept at all. She had been busy plotting; somehow, she would find a way to join the company. With half the city garrison on the march, surely there was no need to fear for her safety.

"If only to see the sea," Adrina called out to the wind, "to smell salt air and wiggle my toes in the sand."

"Wiggle toes in the sand?" asked a voice from behind her.

Adrina quickly brushed her hair back and sat up. "Sorry Lady Isador, I thought I was alone."

"Talking to yourself are you now. You need more fresh air dear. You look peaked. Did you sleep well last night?"

Adrina considered lying. "Not really. It seems the world is passing me by and all I can do is watch. Do you know what I mean?"

Isador sat down on the bed beside Adrina. "You're talking about the departure today aren't you. When I was a girl of sixteen, I wanted to see the whole of the land. Odd though it is, all I want to do now is go home. You see, home is the place you try so very hard to get away from only to miss dearly when you are gone."

"Oh Isador, are you making fun of me?"

"No dear," said Isador taking Adrina's hand, "I'm not. Have you considered simply asking His Majesty?" No, Adrina hadn't. "King Andrew can be very open-minded at times. Look to the Princess Calyin. Your sister traveled more times to the East than I care to count."

"That was because of her betrothal to Lord Serant of the Territories."

"Yes, yes it was, but the Barony of Klaive is not far removed from Alderan City."

Adrina winced. "I do not want my life decided for me like father tried to decide Midori's."

"Your sister's betrothal to King Jarom was purely a matter of state and for the good of Great Kingdom," Isador said with a stern tone. "You may never know His Majesty's anguish over that decision, but I knew, and your mother, bless her soul, knew as well. His Majesty was simply attempting to make amends for a transgression of youth."

"Did my father really win mother's hand over Jarom?"

Isador smiled and brushed back a wayward strand of Adrina's hair. "His Majesty won more than her hand, he won her heart, and when Alexandria came to Imtal, she brought with her Jarom's own heart."

Adrina's eyes wandered to the sunshine playing in the window. "Do you really think he would listen, Isador?"

"You know I do, Young Highness."

***

Adrina awaited her father's response. Despite frowns and stares she maintained a smile.

Father Tenuus, silent and brooding, stood off to King Andrew's right, a sour frown set to his lips. The king frowned likewise, probably agreeing with the captain's statement—the open road and a long, hard journey were no place for a young princess. Still, Father Jacob had added a rare touch. His blessing for her to accompany the group came as a surprise to say the least, and thus was surely the reason for the sour grimace Father Tenuus bore before him.

Andrew rose from his high-backed chair and spread his broad shoulders wide. He looked first to Captain Brodst and then to the two distinguished visitors, Father Jacob and Keeper Martin. "Three years have come and gone since your mother's passing. Each day I grieve. Each day the pain does not diminish, it grows. I am beyond healing Adrina. Queen Alexandria *was* my life. You look so very much like her my dear, sweet Adrina.

"Each day I also see this pain mirrored in your eyes. I ask myself what I can do to end it. Yet, if I cannot ease my own, how can I ease it for another? I think the time away could be the time to finally heal. You may go with my blessing, my dear."

King Andrew looked to Lady Isador, "And, I understand you will visit the Barony of Klaive on the return. You don't know how much that pleases me, my dear. 'Tis a beautiful place come spring. Often I've envied Klaive his place by the great sea. Rudden Klaiveson is an apt and likeable fellow. When you announce your betrothal to him you will have made a wise choice, my daughter."

Adrina began to hurry away. She turned to look back at Lady Isador. "What of you, Lady Isador? I mean, you will come with. You do want to go home, don't you?"

"South Province will have to wait." Lady Isador sighed, looked away. "Hurry along now, before I come to tears. I'll be along in a moment to help you pack."

***

Glowing with delight at her father's approval, Adrina guided her mount through the palace gates, her head held high. She cast thoughts of Rudden Klaiveson away—nothing was going to spoil her day. The Barony of Klaive was at the very least a six-day ride away, and first they would journey to Alderan by the sea.

Adrina rode along the cobbled streets of Imtal toward its southernmost portcullis. She knew she would miss the city. So often had she looked out her window, stared at its tall gray walls, and dreamed of things beyond that the lands beyond seemed just that, a dream. She would miss Lady Isador, her maternal nanny, and her father, Andrew, this was true. But oddly, most of all she would miss those tall gray walls. They had housed and symbolized her fears, her loss, her anger, even her hopes and dreams for so long they truly seemed a part of her. The future without them to look out at, even if only for a few weeks, seemed frightening.

Her dreams had held her and carried her through those three long years. But now she finally had what she wanted and suddenly she felt an overwhelming urge to turn around and race back to Imtal Palace—for there, she could dwell in her dreams and hide from the truth, the cold bitter truth.

"Pleasant thoughts," she whispered, "only pleasant thoughts today."

She let her mind wander along the cobbled city streets and small shadowed alleyways they passed, pieces of her thoughts falling into every nook and cranny.

As the iron grate clambered closed behind her

the excitement of the open road before them, the open green of a large inland plain and the gentle rolling of soft hills in the distance swept her away. She held no remorse for leaving now, only hopes for the thrills that lay ahead.

With but a gentle touch of moisture in it, the air that morning was fresh and cool. Overhead the sky was cloudy and dark and, even though it held the promise of rain, it held an appearance of serenity. Adrina inhaled a deep breath and drank in the early morning aromas—the smell of grass and of early morning dew—then tightened her grip on the reins and bid her horse to speed onward.

Three squadrons of garrison troops filing through the city gates in ponderously long lines, four abreast, had been an awesome spectacle, yet the sound of hundreds of hooves and thousands of feet plodding along muddy ground, filling the air, was equally as spectacular.

"Half the city garrison," Adrina whispered to herself and to the wind, "all headed south, south to Alderan by the sea."

Chapters 5 and 6: Review Questions

1. Does Vilmos like or dislike doing "housework"? Explain.

2. What's the secret place Vilmos visits in his dreams? What's so wrong about going there?

3. What happens when Vilmos confronts the stranger and tells him to show himself?

4. Why does Adrina start to worry about Emel when she hears the trumpets sounding?

5. Why do you think Adrina almost runs to Emel when he returns, but then looks away?

6. What happened to Ridemaster Gabrylle out Braddabaggon Way and why is it funny?

7. What does Lady Isador mean when she says, "Odd though it is, all I want to do now is go home. You see, home is the place you try so very hard to get away from, only to miss dearly when you are gone."

8. Why does Adrina say she doesn't want her life decided for her?

9. Why does King Andrew say he is beyond healing, and that he sees pain in Adrina's eyes?

Words to Watch

Torture	Companion	Somber
Overshadow	Destination	Ration
Vigor	Beguile	Utmost
Nervously	Elude	Gibbous
Stammer	Shaman	Stark
Sympathetic	Saddlebag	Hostile

Chapter Seven: Meeting

Sight had been the first sense to return to Vilmos' tortured world. The other senses followed at a pace of their own accord—except pain. Pain it seemed had always been there, overshadowing the sense of touch. Taste came in the form of a pasty film that covered his tongue, which as he rubbed it away made his stomach sour. A vague odor came to his nostrils, the smell of his own sweat. The last sense to return was hearing. Rapid breathing burst upon him and Vilmos started.

"You are truly the evil one," Vilmos repeated in hushed tones.

The sound of stifled, irregular breaths fell upon his ears again. Realizing the sound was not his own, Vilmos shrank back into the corner. He would not have been amazed to see the dark-faced one sitting beside him—this he expected—yet as he turned, meeting a warm smile, he nearly wet his pants.

"Mi-do-ri, is that you?"

The tutor, seated at a chair next to the bed, stared intently at him. The expression on her face was one that Vilmos did not recognize, one completely out of place, a look not of dismay or terror but of understanding and approval.

Vilmos pinched himself to ensure he wasn't somehow still dreaming, and then asked excitedly, "What are you doing here?"

The teacher answered with words he had not expected. "Watching you, Vilmos," she whispered softly.

In reaction to his anxiety, she shuffled the chair away from him.

"Why didn't you wake me? I was having a terrible, terrible dream. I was probably even talking in my sleep." Vilmos halted only for an instant to intake a breath. "I do that sometimes, just go on and on and on about nothing. The dream was scary, I think."

"Don't be silly," said Midori, "we both know you were not sleeping. I am a friend, Vilmos; there is no need to fear me. I am here to help you."

"Then was it real? Did it really happen?" asked Vilmos with renewed vigor in his words.

Midori glanced at Vilmos' hands and the blood dripping from his shoulders. "If you believe it occurred, then it did. If you believe…"

"I'm afraid," admitted Vilmos, "are you here to take me away?"

"No, Vilmos, I will not take you away, nor will I let the black priests take you away." She moved the chair closer to the bed once more. "I am here to help you."

"I don't need any help. Please just go away," said Vilmos feeling suddenly brave.

"I can't go away Vilmos. You need my help more than you know." Midori glanced nervously out the window. "Vilmos, you are very special. All you have to do is trust me and let me help you. Can you do that?"

Vilmos nodded. Midori touched a dark yellow

stone to the palms of his hands. "It is a healing stone," she said, "it will ease the pain."

"Is it magic?" asked Vilmos warily.

"In a way, perhaps," said Midori, upturning warm green eyes to ease Vilmos' fright, "but this stone comes from the temple of Mother-Earth." The stone began to glow bright yellow, then slowly dulled to charcoal gray. The pain gone from his hands, Vilmos suddenly noticed the sharp throbbing of his shoulders. "I am sorry. The stone's power is gone, but I could not have undone that anyway. I must go now. Will you come with me?"

"Wh-wh-where," stammered Vilmos, "are you going?"

"I am going to meet someone. A very good friend, who is special like you. He has waited a long time for you to be ready."

An internal voice told Vilmos if he were to leave now he would never be coming home again. "Midori, I am afraid."

The gentle woman offered Vilmos her hand and hesitantly he accepted. Her touch, sympathetic and soothing, put Vilmos more at ease. He looked up into her soft green eyes and suddenly worries and reservations about her intentions faded away. He would go wherever she would take him.

"We have to move swiftly," Midori said as she led him from the house. "The woods are a strange enough place with the light of day, let alone without it."

They had just reached the edge of the village when the sound of drums burst into the air. Midori began to run all out, dragging Vilmos behind her. "Hurry, hurry," she said. "They come."

They made the trek from the village to the dark wood at a record pace, Midori dragging Vilmos behind her. Coming to a path, they took it. It was a seldom-used path, so it was largely overgrown with weeds and underbrush, but still visible to an observant eye.

High overhead the sky was turning dark and yet they followed the little trail. Many questions flooded into Vilmos' young mind. Where were they going? What of his mother and father? What of the bear? What of the drums?

Several times he tried to speak, though no words ever escaped his lips. He simply followed as Midori led him along the tangled trail, holding tightly to her hand. A sickness was welling up from his stomach. He felt the whole of the world was suddenly somehow different and the feeling didn't end as the trail did, coming to an abrupt end near the forest's edge.

The two emerged from the forest's shadowed darkness. The sun had already sunk low on the horizon in front of them. Soon it would be night. A large meadow spread beyond the forest's veil and soon they found themselves trudging across it. Vilmos could not see beyond the meadow's brink due to the rolling hills beyond it. He wondered what they would find on the other side, or perhaps if their destination lay beyond the hills, somewhere off in the unseen distance.

Determined now to quietly follow his silent companion, trudging on tired and sore feet, Vilmos began to wonder if they would ever stop to rest or sleep. His answer came as they marched up into the soft, rolling foothills beyond the meadow. They quickly found themselves on a rocky precipice overlooking the most beautiful sight Vilmos had ever seen—the deep valley of his imagining.

"Hello Vilmos," simply stated a strangely familiar voice.

Vilmos was startled by the sudden appearance of the other. He stared at the peculiar, tiny man for a time. His skin was the color of rough leather; the face deep set with wrinkles that covered its entirety was the best indicator of his great age; hair long and black with whispers of gray neither accented nor subtracted from his appearance of age and wisdom. Vilmos stared into eyes as silver as the moonlight, and found the man had a special energy about him. It seemed like an inner flow of light and it intrigued Vilmos, and perhaps beguiled him.

Vilmos finally responded with a timid, "Hul-lo."

"I am Xith," spoke the man in a clear unwavering tone, "shaman of the great North Reach, perhaps the last of my kind, the last of the Watchers."

"How do you... Watchers? There is no such thing as a Watcher. That is only legend."

"Ahh, yet here I stand before you and you better than anyone else should know it to be true."

Vilmos searched his mind. The words appeared to be true, but how could it be so. The tiny man who stood before him could not possibly be a Watcher—Vilmos quickly discarded the thought. He would not judge others so hastily anymore. He had already learned his lesson once before about incorrectly judging people.

In the history written down in the Great Book, he recalled mention of the Watchers. He closed his eyes and concentrated, trying to find the words that momentarily eluded him. "...and the Watchers shall return from their long vigil. They shall bring word of the Coming..."

Vilmos opened his eyes. "You do not look like one of the great Watchers. You look more like a gnome than anything else."

Xith paused and took a deep breath. "Gnomes have not been seen in the land since Father Gnome sealed Solstice Mountain five hundred years ago."

"Father Gnome and Queen Elf are dead," said Vilmos, "and Oread was cast to the four winds with her siblings."

Xith sat and motioned for Vilmos to do likewise. He said nothing for a time afterward and simply stared at the boy, then spoke. "History belongs to the teller and is only as reliable as the teller's recollection of it."

Far off Vilmos heard the sounding of drums again. He saw Midori nervously glance to the woods. "Why are you here?" Vilmos asked.

"You already know the answer."

"Huh? I do?" said Vilmos without thinking. He slapped a hand to his mouth and raised his eyebrows. A realization entered his mind. He remembered something that had been gnawing at him ever since he had heard the shaman's voice. He had almost recalled it before, but he had lost the thought. Now, he did remember. He knew what had been lost in his subconscious. "You were there last night, in my dream and again before. I saw you."

"Yes," Xith said.

"Then was it all real?"

"It was very real, more real than you will ever know." Xith leaned forward and touched a hand to Vilmos' shoulder; the raked flesh was already beginning to fester. The shaman shook his head in disgust.

"But, but how... How did you... and now you are here... Thank you!" exclaimed Vilmos, clutching Xith's hand. "I remember now. I remember it all. I have seen you often in my dreams."

"I did only that which I must," Xith's voice was calm, unchanged.

"What do you want of me? Why have you returned?" Vilmos searched for a clue that would somehow indicate the shaman's intent. He continued to gaze into the shaman's eyes, and a feeling of exhilaration swept over him.

"We will camp here tonight. Get some rest Vilmos," said Xith, "tomorrow I will answer your questions. *Do not worry, for there is nothing to worry about. All fears are behind you for a time.* You will *sleep* peacefully this night. *Sleep*, young Vilmos."

Overcome with sudden fatigue, Vilmos found a dire need for sleep. Xith motioned with his hands and a fire appeared. Its warmth carried with it a healing touch and as soon as Vilmos lay down on the hard ground next to the fire, he fell asleep.

***

"Midori, come here. Let me look at you," said Xith, after a brief lull, "it has been a long time since I last saw you."

Xith stretched out his hands to greet Midori's. The two took a seat beside the fire opposite Vilmos. Xith's silver eyes glowed with joy in the firelight. He was obviously pleased at how Midori had grown. The years had surely developed her.

"Yes it has. I have not seen you since that day long ago when you left my dreams. I was only a child then," somberly stated Midori.

"Yes, you were. You have grown into a fine woman and have learned very well. I am proud of you," said Xith matter-of-factly. His words of praise the absolute truth. He was indeed proud of her achievements, although he was not completely surprised by them. He had seen great promise in her when he had chosen her.

Midori's lips rose into a knowing smile. Xith had been her greatest mentor. She respected him deeply for it and held his approval in the highest regard. "Thank you, Master Xith. I am honored by your kind words. Do we go together to Tsitadel'?"

"No, I am afraid the circumstances have changed. I must take Vilmos with me. There is another that I must take to the secret city, one with greater need. But that is not for some time now. There is much to be done before then, so much to be done before then..." his voice trailed off. He heard drums sounding in the distance again.

Midori honed in solely on the one part of the statement that struck her as inconceivable. "With you? Not with the others?" she asked, a spark of fear entering her mind.

"Yes, I am afraid so. You should return now, there is much to do. We will meet again soon. Do not fret. There is nothing to worry about. Just explain to the council that I was wrong."

"But, you've never been wrong." Midori didn't know how she could tell the council Xith had been in error. No one would believe her. She knew something was drastically wrong, and an alarm sounded in the corners of her mind, though she tried to remain calm.

"I am an old man and old men should be allowed an occasional misjudgment. Besides times are changing. Tell them, I know they will believe you. *Mention nothing of what you have seen. Clear the thoughts from your mind. Believe in me, Midori. What I do is for the best,*" said Xith, his words flowing freely.

"I do believe in you, my friend. I will do what you say." Midori took his hand and added with an emotion-filled voice, "I will not fail you."

"Please go. And take my blessing with you."

"I will worry about you my friend," Midori said. "Will you be safe?"

"My child," began Xith, using a soft-handed tone, "of course I will come to no harm. *There is no need to worry.* Time is short dear Midori. I have a great deal to say. Listen well."

A short pause followed while the words echoed in Midori's mind, *there is no need to worry.*

"Promise me you will forget what you know and what you have seen. Think of the boy no more. He is under my care. This alone should ease your woes. A great change is sweeping across the land. Great events are beginning to unfold. Things even I can only wonder at. The Kingdom of Sever is no longer safe. Do not return here.

"Take my mount. In the saddlebags, you will find several weeks of dried rations and three scrolls. The first must go to Master T'aver, you should know where to find him and yes, dear, I recall your dread of the swamp. I have inscribed that scroll with a special seal. The seal can only be broken by his hand.

"Still, choose your messenger with utmost care. *This message must reach his hands.* He *must* know what to do when the time comes. The second scroll you are to read only after you have departed the council. *Do not read it before then.* Among its instructions it lists the time when you should open and read the final scroll. *Under no circumstances are you to read it before the appropriate time.*

"Go now and take my blessing with you, it is for you that I fear the most." Xith's face grew dark and shadowed. "Watch your way with care, and I will see you many more times."

"Many more times," Xith repeated, waving to Midori as she departed. Then he looked to the heavens and sighed.

Nestled among a few shining stars under an otherwise cloudy sky, a pale and somber gibbous moon shone down. He bedded down beneath his thick blanket, his worries turning from the girl who ran away into the stark, hostile unknown to the boy, Vilmos, who was cradled in the known.

Taking the boy to Tsitadel' would have proven the easiest route, though he had already followed this path to its end in his mind. No, this path was reserved for another.

Xith had other plans for the boy, and in this he must not fail. He did not know if he could cheat fate, or even if it was wise to try, but try he must.

Chapter 7: Word Search

Can you find these words in the puzzle?

Nervously	Elude	Gibbous	Journey
Sympathetic	Saddlebag	Hostile	Adrina
Overshadow	Destination	Ration	Mystery
Torture	Companion	Somber	Friends
Stammer	Shaman	Stark	Nanny
Vigor	Beguile	Utmost	Action
King	Sun	Lamp	Joy

T	P	E	O	A	V	M	N	W	E	W	S	K	L	M	I	B	C	W	Z
B	E	R	Y	H	Z	Q	U	I	K	O	T	E	G	B	N	C	Z	M	N
A	F	U	J	O	H	R	R	O	M	I	A	E	M	A	D	R	I	N	A
T	A	T	D	Y	C	D	W	B	S	S	M	T	U	B	C	B	N	B	G
S	G	R	J	E	Y	Z	E	Q	J	K	M	L	C	T	E	W	I	O	I
O	S	O	S	E	S	R	U	C	I	T	E	H	T	A	P	M	Y	S	B
M	A	T	T	H	B	T	N	L	R	F	R	H	X	B	N	F	D	A	B
T	K	I	N	G	R	E	I	O	P	W	O	D	A	H	S	R	E	V	O
U	H	O	S	T	I	L	E	N	D	Z	X	B	R	T	A	Y	U	G	U
C	V	O	P	R	O	J	T	N	A	N	N	Y	E	N	D	J	Y	E	S
G	X	I	N	R	Y	J	E	E	I	T	P	B	A	D	D	W	E	L	S
L	A	N	G	R	E	O	G	R	H	Y	I	M	X	E	L	R	F	I	M
Z	R	M	G	O	S	U	W	V	U	B	A	O	B	J	E	E	I	U	L
W	A	R	R	I	R	R	V	O	S	H	J	U	N	G	B	X	K	G	P
T	T	I	N	Y	N	N	O	U	S	E	F	J	R	Z	A	W	R	E	M
S	I	G	N	O	F	E	F	S	Y	R	T	U	O	R	G	D	R	B	A
G	O	B	I	J	O	Y	S	L	H	A	M	Y	S	T	E	R	Y	E	L
M	N	T	T	P	T	E	A	Y	C	X	Z	E	L	U	D	E	B	R	N
S	C	O	M	P	A	N	I	O	N	A	D	R	S	G	R	E	T	H	U
A	S	D	N	I	E	R	F	H	J	K	R	E	A	O	K	R	A	T	S

Words to Watch

Guidance	Monotonous	Raucous
Occasional	Subordinate	Reprieve
Dismount	Distinguish	Flatter
Communicate	Dishearten	Embarrassment
Predecessor	Lackluster	Proposition
Aftertaste	Apprenticeship	Influence
Petty	Flagging	Traitor

Chapter Eight: Guidance

The storm clouds of early morning were blown south by strong winds out of the north and a clear bright sky quickly replaced dark clouds. Adrina rode quietly, content for a time simply to watch the scenery they passed, scattered trees, farmers and work animals in fields, and the occasional traveler. The swelling rounds of the Braddabaggon quickly replaced the green of flat open plains. Though the gentle foothills weren't wild country, Adrina kept her eyes wide open. She didn't want to end up like Ridemaster Gabrylle. No lowland cat was going to ruin her day.

She thought about the long southwesterly trek to Alderan. The coastal port city, a mere day's ride south of the Free Cities of Mir and Veter, was rumored to be beautiful beyond compare. In days of old Alderan City had been the capital of the Kingdom. Named after the first king of the land, the Alder, it was once considered the meeting place of the North, South and East.

Adrina maneuvered her mount between Keeper Martin and Emel, and attempted to spark a conversation with Emel, though without success. She didn't know why he was angry with her but she aimed to apologize quickly. She needed someone to talk to.

"Emel, I am sorry. I won't do it ever again, whatever it was. I promise," said Adrina softly.

"Are you at least going to tell me what you know?" Emel asked. "Or do I get nothing in repayment?"

Before she might have decided to come clean and admit she didn't know anything, but as she considered his question, she decided instead to feed him along. "Well, you actually didn't help me. It was Father Jacob who did, and he already knows the plan."

In response, Emel spurred his mount and rode to the front of the party. Her intent hadn't been to anger Emel, only to carry on a conversation with him. Now she felt doubly poor for what she had done. An earlier promise would be kept, she would say an extra prayer this evening to repent for the subterfuge.

"Dear, he will forgive you in time. For now, just let him be. Enjoy the morning and the fresh air. Drink in its beauty," said Keeper Martin.

Adrina was aghast; the Lore Keeper had spoken to her. She didn't have the heart to tell him that she had already enjoyed the morning and was now becoming extremely bored. Her reply instead was an easy response of agreement, a few more hours of silence would be tolerable, but just barely so. She hoped Emel would speak to her soon.

At midday Captain Brodst called the column to a halt. The abeyance would only be long enough to give horses and tired foot soldiers a much needed rest and to grab a light repast. Adrina was very pleased to rid her bottom of the saddle for a short time. After dismounting and leading her horse to where Keeper Martin, Father Jacob and a few others were gathered next to a small stream beside the road, she readily dove into her saddle bags. To her delight, she found dried beef, still-warm rolls and a skin of kindra-ale. In all the excitement she had not even remembered to eat this morning.

While she ate, Adrina looked to the Lore Keeper and the king's first minister. She wondered at Father Jacob's approval of her presence. His words had surprised her then and puzzled her now as she contemplated them. Why did a man who spoke directly to Great-Father care about a mere girl? Why did a man like that do anything?

And then there was Keeper Martin. Rumor had it the great keepers communicated in dreams and that is how they recorded the histories of all that went on in the land. Rumor also had it that Martin was unlike his predecessors. Martin was forever traversing the land. Heading over-mountain, braving the wilds of the Territories or journeying to unknown places in the Far South. Before Martin the head keeper never left the Halls of Knowledge.

"It is impolite to stare, dear," whispered a voice in her ear.

Hastily, Adrina swallowed a lump of half-chewed meat. "I didn't mean to stare. Do you know everything, Keeper?"

Grey-haired Martin chuckled. "No, Your Highness, I don't, though there are those who say I would like to."

Adrina took a sip of kindra-ale, a bitter tasting drink with an unpleasant aftertaste that was strangely satisfying. "Will you be going all the way to Alderan with us, Keeper Martin?"

"I was planning to turn south at the crossroads and press on to South Province with the detachment heading to Quashan' garrison, but I think I will continue to Alderan. My business in the South can wait a few days."

Not knowing what else to say, Adrina smiled and returned to her meal. After eating she wandered to the edge of the stream. There was a small pool here, formed where white waters rushing from upstream found themselves blocked by two large boulders. Bending down, she dipped her hands into the water of the pool. Finding it clear, she rinsed the dirt of the road from her face and neck. Then she slipped off her riding boots and dangled her toes in the cool water.

She looked back to the soldiers milling about on the road and finding not a few stares directed her way she blushed. "Not a proper thing to do," she imagined Lady Isador telling her. She quickly slipped her boots back on and pulled the collar of her riding blouse into place.

"Adrina?" called out Emel timidly, approaching slowly. "I'm really sorry about earlier. I was just frustrated that's all. I heard the news about your upcoming betrothal to Rudden Klaiveson. I guess I was just being petty. After all, you are a grown woman, but I thought you would've told me first. We are friends, aren't we?"

"Heard it from your father no doubt." Adrina frowned. "I'm not betrothed to Rudden Klaiveson. I'm to visit Klaive—there's a difference."

"Is there?"

Adrina glared. "Rudden Klaiveson is days away and at the end of our journey. We'll have no talk of him or anyone else that'll ruin our fun, deal?"

Emel nodded in fast agreement.

Hearing the heated discussion of a large group of men, Adrina turned. "What are they discussing over there?"

"Scouts. They left the group a few hours ago.

Must've just returned," replied Emel. He cocked his head in their direction. "Sounds like they're worried about something ahead. The rains returning perhaps. You see the three approaching just now, with the gold lapels?"

"Captains?"

"The one on the right with the grizzled beard is Captain Trendmore. The tall southerner is Captain Adylton. The other is Captain Ghenson. He's quick-witted. I like him."

Adrina grabbed Emel's arm. "Were they just talking about the ship from Wellison?"

"I don't think so. It wouldn't be a prudent thing to do—" A horn sounding the end of the rest cut Emel short. "—Time to mount. Do you wish to ride with me? I can show you a few things, about riding and scouting."

Adrina puckered her lower lip and bit the corner of it. "Really?" she said wide-eyed.

***

With the afternoon came autumn rains . At first it was only a gentle mist coming down upon them, later heavy sheets of icy rain. The travelers quickly became bogged down in gooey, sticky muck. With no place to hide and wait out the storm in the open fields, stopping served no purpose. For safety's sake the great column slowed to a crawl, yet Captain Brodst kept the group traveling onward.

Despite hood and cloak pulled tightly around her, Adrina was drenched through. Rain streamed down her face and though she was drenched, she was happy—the dreariness was comforting and reassuring.

"Isn't this great?" shouted Emel, raising his voice above the ruckus of hundreds of hooves plodding through thick trail mud and the heavy downpour. "Castle watch is monotonous when compared to this, nothing compares to this!"

Adrina edged her mount closer to his, then reached over and slugged him on the arm. Emel didn't respond. He just smirked rather broadly.

Wet clothes and wet saddle began to chaff as time slipped away. Adrina could feel the cold in her bones now and desperately wanted to stop for another rest. She turned to look back at the others through the shroud of rain. Father Jacob wore a solemn, thoughtful expression on an otherwise expressionless face. Knowing that the good priest was always like this—true feeling hidden on the interior of a hardened exterior—she wondered what feelings were hidden behind the clear, impressionless mask. For therein lies the heart of the man—her mother had told her that once long ago.

The rain notwithstanding, Keeper Martin had his eyes wide open. He scanned the horizon ahead. His face, with upturned eyebrows and slightly furled lips, showed little complacency. Clearly he didn't like the rain or the trail conditions, yet as always he sought to maintain a clear awareness of their surroundings and find the good in ill. Something troubled him, noted Adrina. She guessed that it probably had something to do with their journey—the keeper had too much wisdom sometimes.

Besides the ever-present scowl, Captain Brodst had an otherwise expressionless countenance. For Adrina, the scowl signified order. The captain kept his companions and his subordinates in check with it—the guards, the soldiers, not even the distinguished guests, Adrina included, dared to speak their thoughts. They would endure the rain for as long as the captain ordered.

The others in the long line of garrison soldiers fore and aft, still four abreast on the muddied kingdom road, and the palace guardsmen that encircled her, Adrina noted, were disheartened. The rain was bogging down their thoughts. Some of those whose faces she could see despite the murky rain were thinking of other places—perhaps home and loved ones, perhaps just the local ale house—but still it was clear they were thinking of someplace else.

Her special talent, a learned talent for knowing what others were thinking from their expressions, a gift perfected during numerous court sessions, ended as she turned to regard Emel. She had a hard time discerning his feelings from his expressions. This especially troubled her and attracted her to him. As she considered this, her eyes wandered toward him once more—quickly turning away down the muddied path as her gaze met his. The message in his eyes, mixed feelings—feelings she didn't like—was confusing.

As the rain persisted and the day grew long, Captain Brodst signaled another slackening of the pace. Afterwards, he signaled the young sergeant to fall in place beside him. Adrina followed, then after slowing her mount, she did her best to listen in.

"… Remember it will be a light camp, no tents, " reminded the captain, "so find us a good thick spot in a forested canopy."

To Adrina's surprise, he addressed her next.

"Sorry Your Highness," Captain Brodst said, "we will be unable to reach an inn. I had hoped we would be able to make up some time, but the rain is slowing us to a crawl. Our file is too long to risk much faster travel."

"You considered stopping at an inn," said Adrina, more to herself than to the captain. "Even after what you said before we departed Imtal?"

"Come on, Adrina!" yelled Emel, as he urged Ebony to race the wind. "Catch up!"

Captain Brodst was part way into a response that was quickly drowned out as Adrina raced to intercept the retreating figure. She did toss him a final probing stare, though, as she swatted her horse to speed the weary animal's lackluster pace. She was also quick to turn back to the trail ahead as the captain sought to raise an objection. She was certain she was right about his constant scowl. It was his shield.

"You see, my father…" shouted Emel, looking back over his shoulder as his horse galloped through the thick mud and rain, "… the captain has a heart after all."

For a long time the two sped along the trail despite the greatly reduced visibility from the rain, diminishing daylight and their speed. Adrina had a difficult time maintaining her focus on the figure ahead. Soon she became completely unaware of her surroundings, and watched only for the spray of mud from hastening hooves ahead.

"Emel, wait up! We aren't in that much of a hurry are we? The others are well behind us by now. Besides, how can we find a suitable place to stop if we can't even see what we are passing by?"

Emel reined Ebony in. "I don't need to see where I am going. Even in the rain I know this section of the road like the back of my hand." He stroked Ebony Lightning. "My first apprenticeship was as a king's messenger. I know exactly where we'll find a sheltered site away from the rain."

"Then why are we racing?"

"Imtal Palace Guardsmen and guests shall have the base fire. The garrison troops will have to fend for themselves. They have their own detachment and squadron commanders. It is my father's way of telling the palace guard he cares. Garrison soldiers will also see him as one who cares well for his own and perhaps there will be more than a few who at the end of this trip will wish to enlist in his service. At the end of a long journey soldiers remember the little things. Food, water and shelter are held in the highest regard.

"And we race for sport," said Emel urging

Ebony faster and faster.

Mud and dirty water was propelled high into the air and fell just short of Adrina as she fought to catch up with a flagging mount.

After they had rounded several bends in the road and breached several low hills, Adrina momentarily lost sight of Emel. Her heart still pounding from the race, she held her breath as she tried to discern shapes in the dim light. Then she spotted horse and rider racing off the trail and hastened after them.

Just before he reached the edge of the woods, Emel turned Ebony about and raced back toward her. In one swift move he wheeled his mount along side Adrina's and, reaching down, seized her horse's reins just above the bit, bringing the mare to a rigid stop. Not expecting this, Adrina tumbled from the horse into the mud.

Emel dismounted. "Can I help you up, Your Highness?" he asked smugly.

Adrina could see he was trying to contain the humor within from bursting into raucous laughter. Her face was red and tears came to her eyes. Mud clung to her hair, her clothes, her cloak, and frustrated hands did little to remove it. "No, I think you've done enough already. I am quite fine."

Emel tossed her an impish look and if she hadn't burst into laughter, Adrina would have cried deeply. The laughter, a much needed burst of cheer, was oddly cleansing, but short-lived.

"Damn you Emel!" she screamed, "You did this on purpose, didn't you?"

She was crying now and suddenly screaming at him again. "Damn you, damn you—" She realized she was whining and then how pathetic she sounded, and she laughed again—and the laughter felt good.

When Emel offered her his hand in assistance, she pulled him forward, and didn't let go until he landed face first into the mud. Then she tried to run out of his reach, but was too slow.

"Why you," yelled Emel, as he grabbed the retreating foot.

A backwards slip landed her, with a muddled thud, on her backside. She squirmed to get away from him as he dragged her toward him.

"Let me go! Let me go!"

Emel continued to drag her by one leg backwards through the mud as she fought to break free while the rain beat down on them in a sudden strong drove. With both hands, she scooped up a large clump of mud and threw it at Emel. It landed with a splat, squarely on target and she finally broke free of his grip.

"So that's how you want to play it," Emel said, grabbing a large handful of wet muck.

Adrina returned the volley. "Serves you right!"

The mud flinging continued back and forth until they were both drenched and covered in mud from head to toe. Adrina was laughing so hard she fell backwards into the mud, adeptly tripping Emel as she went down. As she pushed a sodden handful into his face, both burst into hearty laughter. Then content to sit idle, allowing the rain to splash down upon them, the two passed a quiet moment.

"Stand up," Adrina said to Emel, offering her hand to him as he stood. "We have to get all this mud off of us before the others catch up. I don't want to get you into any more trouble."

Emel looked at her, eyes agape, as if he had just remembered something that his life depended on. Warily, he accepted her offer, quickly returning to reality from the momentary reprieve. They waited in the rain just long enough for it to wash the majority of the mud from their clothing and then prepared to move under the forest canopy.

"Grab your horse, follow me," said Emel.

Hurriedly, he led her into the large stand of nearby fir.

Quickly the rain became scarcely noticeable as they entered the thick folds of the shielded canopy and as they moved deeper and deeper into the heart of the great fir stand the rain was soon only a pleasant sound in the distance. The world became suddenly quiet and calm.

"Gather some sticks and small branches for kindling. I'll get the larger branches," said Emel. He loosely tied Ebony's reins to a low branch and retrieved an axe from his saddlebags.

Adrina collected dry twigs and small branches into a pile as Emel had asked. When she had finished, Emel had already returned with a plentiful harvest of large branches. A tree had fallen nearby and its great boughs would be put to good use.

After a circle was cleared around where he would start the campfire, Emel quickly assembled the wood into a neat pile with the kindling at the base and the larger branches at the top forming a huddled triangle. Flint and steel were retrieved from saddlebags and an instant later its spark lit the kindling. A few tender puffs spread the tiny flames and soon a gentle fire was crackling, replacing the soft sound of distant rain.

Adrina was almost impressed by his expertise. "Pretty nimble," she said, "how much longer before the others catch up?"

"Soon," Emel said, "so hurry up and take off your clothes. We don't have much time."

Both flattered and outraged, Adrina's face flushed and then became bright red. "What do you mean?" she shouted. She slapped his face. "Why I never! What do you mean get undressed?"

Emel swallowed harshly, then his face turned bright with embarrassment, a close match to the princess'. "What I meant to say was, hurry up and get out of those wet things so we can dry them over the fire."

"Why?" demanded Adrina, still upset.

"I didn't mean it the way it… I mean, what I'm trying to say is…" said a flustered Emel, "You need to dry your things before the others arrive. Otherwise, you know, it might be difficult for you to get them dry. I'll tie a line up between those two trees for you, and then you can hang your clothes to dry. I'll go watch for the others by the trail, just yell when you are finished."

After a moment of silence, Adrina laughed. Now, she understood what he was trying to say. "I'm sorry Emel," Adrina said, quickly adding, "I mean for hitting you, I'm sorry."

The fire was blazing brightly by the time Emel had tied up a secure line. He would have preferred to gather more wood as he should have done, but he didn't. The great fallen tree was close by though, and it could serve as a source for many, many fires to take away the chill of the rainy night.

"Good-bye," he said, "just call out when you're done. If the others get here first I'll call out in greeting to them and you'll know they are close. I'll need to build a watch fire near the forest's edge but that will only take a moment."

***

The watch fire built, Emel was hesitant to leave its warmth. Returning with Ebony Lightning to unsheltered skies seemed an unpleasant proposition and he did so with quick regret. Almost immediately, cold rain drenched any part of him that had been partially dry.

An easterly wind blown from the direction of the distant sea made the rain feel that much colder. He knew, even on an evening such as this, the red glow of the watch fire from the darkened wood cutting into the darkened land could be seen from a long distance. He needn't wait here on the trail for the others, for they could have easily followed the building light to its source. Here he felt safer, safer because he was away from the young princess and the desires of his own young heart.

Safer? he asked himself, immediate alarms sounding in his mind. He had just left Princess Adrina alone in the woods. He had not checked for signs of other passersby. Nor had he checked for signs of other creatures seeking shelter from the rain.

He mounted Ebony and charged into the thick woods, passed the watch fire, ducking low hanging branches as he went. Dark silhouettes of trees passed by in blurs as he raced for the red of the base fire. Reaching the base fire, he found the hollow under the canopy empty.

"A-dri-na, Adrina?" he screamed, his mind filling with dread.

Hastily, Emel dismounted. Panic mandating his every move, he began a frantic search.

"Adrina, where are you?"

For an instant, he felt a breath of air on his neck—perhaps the wind from beyond the forest. Then a hand clasped firmly to his mouth.

"Do not scream. I will not harm you," whispered a dark figure, whirling him around so he was left staring into heavy gray eyes. "We bring word from land and people."

The figure then led Emel deeper into the forest. Emel counted the figures in the shadows as he was led passed them, twelve in all. He soon found himself in a large circle of dark-robed figures. All save one had the hoods secured, masking their faces. Princess Adrina sat in the middle of the circle beside a tall light-haired woman. Dark skin said the woman was surely a southerner, but the light blonde hair seemed out of place.

"Who is your friend?" asked the woman of Adrina, not turning to look at Emel.

"He is the son of the captain of the Imtal guard."

"Sit, Emel Brodstson," said the woman, beckoning with her hand. Then to Adrina she said, "We do not have long, I can hear the column approaching. I must speak fast."

Emel heard nothing save soft rain and perhaps wind.

"Travel not to Alderan by the sea. The ship you seek from Wellison will not arrive. You are in grave danger princess. A great evil has put its mark upon you. It is good you have a friend who cares for your welfare. You would be wise to care as much for yourself."

Adrina glanced at Emel, then asked, "Why me?"

"The struggle is long and many are its participants. The journey you have embarked upon is but the first step along the path. The evil has chosen you because of your position of influence and because of the emptiness within you."

"Can I not rid myself of this mark?"

The woman began speaking more swiftly now. "Look to two strangers for aid, for fate brings them to you. Beware those that are not what they seem and the traitor. A traitor among you will insist you continue to Alderan when it seems you should not. Remember, only death awaits in Alderan."

Adrina regarded the woman and started to say something but Emel cut her off. "What is so important about this ship from Wellison? Why should we even listen to you? You should flee before the garrison soldiers find you and run you through."

"Speak not words in haste, oft you may regret the reply. Yet if this is what you truly wish to know, I will tell you. Know there is a heavy price. Once a thing is known, you may not so easily turn away." The woman paused and stared into Emel's eyes, seemingly pleased with what she saw, she continued. "The ship from Wellison has a most precious cargo, the heir to the throne of Sever. At this very moment, King Charles lies dying in his bed. An assassin's poison is slowly eating away at him. Alas there is no cure, a terrible poison it was.

"The evil uses King Jarom's lust for power just as it uses you and many others. He sees himself seated in the throne room of Imtal Palace. He means to plunge the kingdoms into war. To be sure, he will use the death of Charles and the fears of the heir to his own ends."

"Can I not rid myself of this evil?" repeated Adrina.

"Please leave us now," said the woman to Emel, "go to your watch fire. The soldiers are near. I would speak to Adrina alone."

Emel hesitantly turned away, his pace just slow enough to hear their continued whispers.

"The evil brings the change you so wished for. It has found a home in the emptiness of your heart. You care too little for those around you. You see not the servants who toil for you, workers in the fields on their hands and knees with the whip at their backs, drudges scouring the kitchen floors—"

"I am not heartless," protested Adrina.

"Did I say heartless?" asked the woman. "Tell me, what is the name of the servant girl who cares so much for you that she remains awake through the night to re-stoke your hearth only to feel the lashings of a whip at her back the next day for laziness?"

Adrina fumbled for a name. "She is a servant girl, nothing more."

"Myrial," whispered Emel.

"Queen Alexandria, your mother, would have shed tears at the hearing. Your position has made you forget there are others in the land that suffer. Your father is not the strong and caring king he once was. Fault him not; there are those who use his grief to their own ends. You must open your eyes."

Adrina tried to raise an objection. The lady continued. "Go now. Look for the two strangers, find the son of Charles, beware the traitor and those that are not what they seem. Say nothing of our conversation to anyone."

"But what can I do? I cannot rouse the southern garrisons to arms."

"I did not say to rouse the garrisons. Would you so foolishly provoke war?" The woman paused and stared into the shadows. "And Emel Brodstson, if you have heard enough, continue on your way. Remember, there is always a heavy price."

Chapters 7 and 8: Review Questions

1. Who is waiting for Vilmos when he returns from the strange encounter in the valley, and what happens afterward?

_____

_____

_____

2. Where does Midori take Vilmos, and why does he think he won't be going home again?

_____

_____

_____

3. Why does Xith say, "History belongs to the teller and is only as reliable as the teller's recollection of it."?

_____

_____

_____

4. Why does Emel ride away from Adrina?

_____

_____

_____

5. Why are soldiers staring at Adrina when she goes to the edge of the stream?

_____

_____

_____

6. What happens when Emel and Adrina ride away from the column? Do you think that was a smart thing to do given the circumstances?

_____

_____

_____

7. Who do Adrina and Emel meet in the forest, and what do they learn?

_____

_____

_____

8. Who is Myrial, and why does the lady ask Adrina about her?

_____

_____

_____

Words to Watch

Escort	Foremast	Ironic
Blockade	Lateen	Instantaneous
Engulf	Galleon	Ferocity
Boatswain	Broadside	Laceration
Engagement	Rend	Founder
Dedicated	Grapple	Yearn

Chapter Nine: Ambush

What do we do now Brother?

We die, Brother Galan, Seth said coldly, simply, *but not until we fight honorably and die honorably.*

All eyes keyed to the hulking masses of multi-sailed vessels that hungrily approached.

Cagan? Seth directed the thought to the mind of the ship's captain. *We must get through. We cannot fight them all at once. Can we make it to open water?*

"Perhaps, if we use the escort ships as decoys while we break through—a hard strike to the right side of the blockade should do it. We can try to circle them and make for open seas. Once there, with the wind in our sails, this ship can outrun anything they can throw at us." Cagan spoke aloud as was his chosen fashion.

Running is pointless, Bryan said. *It would only show that we are cowards. We should strike the enemy head on, with our eyes wide open.*

I agree, Galan said.

After a tug at his grizzled beard and a scratch at his large rounded head, Sailmaster Cagan said, "We are not running, but surviving."

You are wrong, Bryan said.

Cagan's open thoughts streamed to Seth who stood beside him. Seth had passed more than a few nights sailing the canals of Kapital with the kind sailmaster. They knew each other well, he knew no one whose love and respect for the sea was greater. It was Cagan's life. He also knew the venerable captain would not let them down, would not let him down, would not let Queen Mother down. *No,* Seth said, *Sailmaster Cagan is not wrong. Go ahead with your plan. I trust your judgment.*

Sailmaster Cagan passed instructions to the ship's broadcaster who in turn relayed them to the escort ships. A maneuver was dealt out to their small, honest fleet—one that would cost them greatly. The escort ships turned sail from their current position, and headed directly into the enemy blockade. They struck hard and to the right side as instructed and in a few terrible, fate-filled minutes, they were overswept. A heavy toll would be brought for their fall, Seth knew this.

Sailors from both sides were washed over the decks. Tiny specks leaping from tiny ships, images that floated farther and farther away. Seth looked down to the deck of the Lady L. Those of the Red were lost in silent meditation, a thing Seth did not presently allow for himself. He knew well why they closed their minds to the screams they perceived—screams of pain, anguish and demise. He knew they were preparing for battle, a battle they must win.

Dark pillars of smoke and flames rose into the air far behind them. Seth saw tiny white sails engulfed in those deadly, dark flames and dark shapes, the broken hulls of fallen ships, sinking into the waiting, black waters. *They found open seas, but at what cost?*

***

Of the many enemy ships that had formed the

blockade, only two were able to raise full sails and remain in proximity to them. The chase was on.

A master at the helm, Cagan turned sails to catch maximum benefit from the winds. He guided the ship into the head of the gull, a maneuver that would eventually steal the draft from the sails of the pursuers as they closed in, and force them to scramble to catch a fresh breeze.

Clever, Sailmaster Cagan, very clever, said Seth.

Cagan's retort was swift and his eyes never broke away from the sails or the wheel. "I had some help did I not?"

The forces of the Mother are at the call of all who know how— A peculiar sight caught Seth's eye and for an instant his thoughts broke off. *—who know how to use them.*

The wind ebbed on the fore-and-aft rigged vessel, which forced them to lose some much-needed speed. Meanwhile, the enemy cutters had finally found their sails and were gaining.

"They will not catch us, they cannot catch us," said Cagan as much to himself as to Seth, "not a chance, not a chance."

"Bo's'n!" he yelled, "Tighten that riggin', attend to that rope, check the trim."

The boatswain's response was loud and shrill. In brief, precise thoughts, he spit out the orders and, in short order, the swift craft lurched forward under proper sails.

Cagan, to the east, look!

A single ship grew from a speck along the horizon in front of them to a dot on the water. They could not afford an engagement now. The pursuers were too close behind.

"It is over, my friend," Cagan said, "one way or another, we must move to engage, either to the rear or front..." The wily sea captain paused. "Yet, perhaps—Yes, if we tack directly toward them we will surely catch them off guard."

Yes, maybe we can gain the upper hand before the others join the match, said Seth with twisted hope.

Cagan ordered the vessel turned against the wind, their nimble sloop could cut well in the tack. The cutters behind them, on the other hand, were much slower in the turns.

Cross-winded the Lady L rapidly approached the ship that a short time ago had been but a mere, distant speck. All on board readied for the inevitable. Silent prayers were sent to Father and Mother to protect and watch over them and to keep them.

Seth looked down at his small group of dedicated followers. He knew that each prepared their mind and spirit for the end. Death was not a fear, but failure was. To pass in such a way would mean dishonor and disgrace. Therefore, they must succeed.

Readily their nimble sloop approached the oncoming vessel with expectant hopes that its captain would not expect a direct assault.

"Captain, she has square foremasts and two lateen rears," yelled the lookout from his perch.

An expression of dismay and fear passed over Cagan's face. He had not expected so great an adversary. The speed with which the vessel had moved through the water had led him to believe it was another cutter. He had not expected a full-sized galleon. His fears permeated the air, and flowed to Seth.

Seth was also worried. King Mark was better prepared than they had thought. He only wished he could contact Brother Liyan and warn him— galleons were not quickly or easily built. Many skilled craftsmen had labored long on such a vessel as they now faced, which, as they drew closer, loomed larger and larger against the pale blue backdrop of the waning day. There could be no turning back now. Fate was locked in.

The two ships, galleon and sloop, were nearly

within striking distance of each other. They were dead on course for the galleon, with the other enemy ships reduced to unseen dots along the horizon to the distant rear. For now, it would be just a one-on-one engagement.

Seth was proud of Cagan's sailors. They held no fear in their thoughts, only determination which was strong and growing with each passing moment. They followed Cagan's orders and kept the sails perfectly trim and rallied for the coming fight.

A questioning voice came into Seth's mind, *Brother Seth?*

Yes, Everrelle, responded Seth curtly. He was angry at the untimely interruption.

Do you mark any of our kind on board their ship?

… I do… not. Seth paused then gasped.

Nor do I, said Galan.

Yes, that is it, my Brothers! There may yet be hope. The enemy may be well prepared but they may also have underestimated the lengths Queen Mother would go through to ensure success. Mere numbers are no match for the power of the Brotherhood.

What if they are merely shielding their thoughts? Bryan said. *We should probe to make sure.*

Seth agreed. Bryan cast his will into the wind. Cagan continued on a direct course for the galleon.

There is no trickery, Bryan said.

Seth smiled, thinking that perhaps the day was not lost.

The galleon captain began to scramble to turn the large ship. He barked out orders, which carried across the darkening waters even above the sound of rising frenzy from both sides. He tried gallantly to fill sails for maneuvering speed though it was a useless effort.

Cleverly, Cagan turned toward the galleon's broadside, the bow of his ship locked straight on the exposed side. With a resonant rending, sloop and galleon collided. The air filled with the cacophony of crunching timbers and shrill screams as the battle was joined.

The galleon had received a potentially lethal blow and was gaining water fast. Still, her sailors would not go down alone. Grapples were swiftly set and tied off tight. The two ships would go down together if the sea had its way.

Cut lines were cast back relentlessly, yet this alone was not enough. Over the bow the enemy forces swept with blades readied in angry hands.

"They do not stand a chance against us!" cried Cagan to his sailors as he swung across to the galleon's low side on a rope tied to the upper rigging.

With a cheer, his men returned his chant and charged, their blades clashed with the enemy, and drew crimson blood.

Still one small group had not moved nor did it seem they had registered the attack. They were the members of the Red and they waited until the mournful screams in their minds reached a crescendo. Then Seth took charge of his fellows and as one they screamed in fury their chant of war, the chant of their ancient brethren.

Blood bathed in rage, they raced forward to the bow, pouring forth like a deadly red rain. A blur of brutal force, they dropped the enemy, each where they stood, with but a single precise touch. Such was their evident anger and the might of their invoked will.

Yet with a cry of ironic agony, their charge ended. Feet no longer tread solely upon enemy dead. Seth felt vivid torment in his soul. The first of the Brotherhood fell, a blow from behind piercing the brother's heart.

Seth vowed to spare no suffering on the one who had delivered the deadly blow. With a jump and a kick, the guilty was knocked stunned to the deck, his demise not instantaneous like the others before him. He would be forced to lie and watch with eyes that were purposefully allowed to move as life slowly dripped away. Seth's blow struck the spinal cord just below the neck on the right side.

Nine and one trudged onward toward the high deck where Cagan now battled the enemy captain. Three sailors were all that remained of his once proud group and they protected his rear as he struggled against the galleon's surly captain. Although thick lines of evident fatigue held to his countenance, Cagan persisted. For now his determination could not be extinguished. Yet the numbers were not on his side and soon the enemy would overwhelm Cagan and the last of his sailors.

Desperately, Seth continued the assault. The enemy was strong and skillfully wielded their weapons. Two more brothers fell.

Seth pushed onward with regained ferocity, as did his companions. He and seven others reached the stairs to the high deck and surpassed them. Only Cagan remained standing, all around him were the dead and the dying, and his sword lay deep in the enemy captain's chest. With the heel of his boot, Cagan smashed downward, and retrieved his cold steel blade. In disgust, he spit into the dead man's face.

Drained, Cagan stumbled. Seth rushed to his aid, and cradled him in still strong arms. "It is only us at the last." Cagan choked on his own blood and weakly added, "... my friend." His clothes blood splattered and shredded revealed multiple lacerations beneath.

There was no time to attend to Cagan's wounds, Seth knew this. The two remaining ships were near, and within minutes their ranks would sweep over the decks toward the place where the last few survivors stood. The middle decks of the sinking galleon were already being claimed by the yearning sea and their own small ship was beginning to founder under the yearning weight. The end was surely near.

Seth spoke to the seven yet fated to remain, words that exited his mind with powerful intent, words that he truly meant. *They are what stand in the way of our victory. We cannot fail! We will not fail! Do not still your fervor, nor your fury. We shall make them pay well beyond their expectations. Eight against the many shall be triumphant!*

"There are... nine!" shouted Cagan.

Chapter 9: Word Sort

Can you rewrite the word list in alphabetical order? Hint: A to Z.

Escort
Blockade
Engulf
Boatswain
Engagement
Dedicated
Foremast
Lateen
Galleon

Can you rewrite the word list in alphabetical order? Hint: A to Z.

Rend
Broadside
Grapple
Ironic
Instantaneous
Ferocity
Laceration
Founder
Yearn

Can you rewrite the word list in reverse alphabetical order? Hint: Z to A.

Incantation
Cacophony
Procession
Unmistakable
Appeal
Enthusiastic
Education
Distinctive
Betray

Words to Watch

Suspicious	Incantation	Forbidden
Descent	Cacophony	Succumb
Punishment	Procession	Destructive
Distinctive	Unmistakable	Knotted
Betray	Appeal	Melancholy
Quotation	Enthusiastic	Whittle
Teleport	Education	

Chapter Ten: First Lessons

Vilmos bolted upright, unsure what had awoken him. Thoughts from the previous day came flooding into his mind. The Shaman. Midori. The drums, he heard the drums again. And voices.

Then for an instant all thought stopped. No dreams, he realized, no dreams. He had slept peacefully during the night and nothing had awoken him, until just now. The drums, he heard them again.

He was about to speak when Xith clamped a hand to his mouth. The shaman stared meaningfully into his eyes. "Not a sound. Take my hand."

Vilmos nodded. His knees were trembling. He sat as Xith indicated he should. Quietly the two waited. The sound of voices and drums grew steadily clearer and closer. Soon it became readily apparent that whoever was out there was in the hills just beyond their clearing.

Vilmos was ready to run but Xith sat very still, his eyes closed, his face pale and drawn, and his hand clasped tightly to Vilmos'. From high overhead came the distant call of a hunter. Staring long, Vilmos caught sight of the grandest eagle he had ever seen. It was circling lazily over the hills and as Vilmos peered up at it, it turned a glistening black eye in his direction.

Suspicious, Vilmos stared at Xith.

The eagle called out again, a long piercing call, and then it folded its powerful wings and dove from the heavens. Vilmos held his breath as he watched it fall. It soared over the cliff's edge and down into the depths of the deep valley.

Color slowly returned to Xith's face and he released Vilmos' hand. "Huntsmen and trackers," he whispered, patting Vilmos on the back reassuringly. "They are from your village and the neighboring two."

Vilmos turned a watchful eye to the hills. "Are they looking for me?"

The shaman shook his head. "As far as I can tell, they hunt an animal of some sort."

"The bear, the black bear," said Vilmos, wide-eyed. "Is it near?"

Xith asked Vilmos to explain. Vilmos told the shaman of the bear attacks, the death of the girl from Olex Village, and his own encounter with one.

"Bears you say," Xith said, "that is interesting. Bears are not easily stirred, nor easily angered. Animals of the forest have a keen sense about them. We will have to keep our eyes open as we move north. To be sure, it would not be wise to travel north through Vangar Forest, and a descent into the valley from here shouldn't be too bad."

Vilmos saw a puzzled expression cross the shaman's face and his eyes darted toward the hills. "You weren't expecting hunters and trackers were you," said Vilmos, sounding suddenly older than his years. "Who were you expecting, shaman?"

"There is no need to trouble over the could-have-beens," replied Xith. "Are you hungry?"

Vilmos agreed he was. The shaman removed a thick slab of finely smoked beef and a loaf of hard black bread from his saddlebags.

"Better eat all you care to," Xith said, "it will be a long day."

"I am going home then?" asked Vilmos. "My parents will miss me if I am not home soon."

Xith had been busily cutting thin strips of beef. He paused, and then laid the knife aside. As he began to speak, his bright and shiny eyes lost their gleam and there was evident sadness in his voice. "Many, many years ago, I made a promise to a young couple who were very much in love. Five years they had been wed and still they had no children. They so wanted a child. I told them of a girl heavy with child in need of caring hands.

"The girl, your mother, needed a secluded place to stay, a place where none knew her or that her child was without a father. Death by stoning is the punishment for such a child and mother.

"I told the couple they must harbor the child's mother and see that the child entered the world without harm. Afterward the child would be theirs to keep and raise as their own. I also told them there was a price. One day I would return for the child. Until that day the child was in their care—"

"—I want to at least talk to my mother," cut in Vilmos. "I'll tell her I am fine and that I am with you. She will understand, though I am sure she will tell you to make sure I am back before the next Seventhday."

"*You will not be home before the next Seventhday, Vilmos, or any other day.*" Xith paused to ensure Vilmos understood. "Your father was among those from the three villages. I could sense his anguish. He knew the day I spoke of those many odd years ago had come. Your feelings for him are wrong you know. He loves you more than the air he breathes.

"I stayed with them for three days when I escaped from the North with your mother. I told them the signs to watch for, the signs that would tell them I would return." Xith stood and walked to the rim of the valley and gazed across the great span. He said nothing for a time, and then turned to look back at Vilmos. "Your magic is what brought me to you, Vilmos, and the reason your father was so exacting. He knew your use of magic would only hasten me to your door."

Tears in his eyes, Vilmos looked away from the shaman.

"*Do not be sad,* young Vilmos. To be sure, Great-Father and Mother-Earth will not let their sacrifice go unrewarded. *Look now to the future* and the days ahead. "—There was a distinctive quality to the spoken speech that was consciously inaudible to all save cautioned ears, this was the power of Voice, and Xith played upon its dominion with the touch of a maestro's hand.—"*In your heart, you have always known* one day *you would leave your home.* You *know* this is true."

Vilmos nodded in agreement. Closing his eyes, he pictured long black hair touched with gray and tired eyes of hazel.

Xith turned to fully face Vilmos and stared directly into his eyes. "It is time we started our journey. There is much to do, so very much to do. I would ask you now to come into my service—a sort of apprenticeship. There is much I can teach you of the powers within you. I would have you enter my service of your own free will but there are things I must first tell you.

"Know that you *can* stay if that is your intent. Know also, the dark priests will surely find you. They will not be as kind as I. They will bring a sentence of death upon those you love, as that is the law."

Vilmos shuddered at the mention of the dark

priests. Their task was to purge the land of magic, a task they and those that served them had carried out across the centuries.

"Or you can come with me now. I will do my best to teach you control over your powers. And though I am not human, I *can* teach you the way of the Magus." Xith's expression became stern. "A very difficult trial awaits in the coming days. In this I need your help, Vilmos. Will you help me?"

"Lillath will be lonely," Vilmos said, wiping tears away from wet cheeks. "Will they ever have another child?"

"In time, Lillath *will* have a child."

"What of the dreams, are they gone?"

Xith stared directly into Vilmos' eyes. "Have you made your choice, Vilmos?"

"I wish to go with you."

Xith's face betrayed no emotion, pleased or otherwise. He waved his hand, beckoning Vilmos to follow him.

***

The descent into the deep valley had taken hours. Picking their way along the broken trail to the valley's floor had been akin to torture. Four times the trail cut into the face of perilously high walls had ended, and four times they had used ropes to continue the descent. Each time Vilmos had muttered under his breath that there had to be other trails and each time Xith had responded with, "Perhaps, perhaps not. At any rate this is the path we have chanced upon." Xith had spoken the words with such vigor that Vilmos was sure there was a lesson in the words, but what it was he didn't know.

Vilmos craned his neck to see the lip of the wall they had just descended. He was panting, and sweat dripped from his chin. Vilmos sighed and fought to take in one lengthy breath to get his breathing under control. The hard work had been oddly cleansing.

A soft breeze cutting through the valley brought cool air swirling beside the wall. Vilmos smiled, cool perspiration against his skin felt good. "Where do we go from here shaman?"

"The northwesterly curve of the valley will carry us to the upper bounds of the Vangar," Xith said, indicating it was time to begin again. The brief rest was over.

The shaman spoke as he walked, "From there, it is at most a day's trek to the plains beyond. We do not want to delay long in the forest. Hearing the news of bear attacks puts me at great unease. For something that surely isn't human or oreadan has taken up residence there."

"Oreadan," mused Vilmos, turning to regard the shaman more closely. With the high sun at his back, the shaman seemed even more intriguing and mystical. Perhaps it was the wrinkled, timeworn face or the troubled, weary eyes that although the sun dulled them were still of a silvery gray. Perhaps his height, which measured Vilmos' equal—but Vilmos was a boy with much growth ahead. As Vilmos considered this, Xith's words struck a chord—nothing was north. "Do you mean to leave Sever? There is nothing but desolation beyond."

"That is what you have been told, this is true. But the whole of the greatest kingdom in all the lands is north," answered Xith, as he slung his leather satchel over the opposite shoulder and changed his walking stick into his left hand.

"The Alder's Kingdom."

"Yes, the Alder's Kingdom, known as Great Kingdom to those who dwell there."

Methodically, Xith picked up his staff and placed it in front of him with each step. Although well in his years, he didn't show the signs of it. He didn't need the walking stick though it looked very appropriate in his hand.

When it seemed Xith would say no more, he

added, "And, the Borderlands are north of course."

"Is that where we will go?" asked Vilmos, "I do not want to go there. I have heard strange tales about the Borderlands—evil dwells there," a direct quotation from his mother. Vilmos was well practiced at recalling such things. His eyes grew wide. "What of the Hunter Clan? What of the Bandit King?"

"We must first enter Great Kingdom at a place called South Province."

***

The first night in the valley they camped beneath the stars. Vilmos learned the deep valley was a harsh place without a warming sun. Soon after dusk, the land lost all its warmth and the cold only worsened during the night.

Two hours before sunrise, they started their solitary march. By the time the evening sun arrived, they hoped to reach the river at the valley's center. If they could cross the river an hour or so before nightfall they could, with luck, dry their clothes by the last of the sun's rays. If they didn't reach the river in time they would camp on the close shore and cross the river the next morning, but this would mean many wasted hours.

Xith set a furiously fast pace. Any rest periods this day would be few and short. Vilmos couldn't be sure, but it seemed the farther north they went the more eager the shaman was to quicken the pace. The sores about his shoulders had grown scabs but still they ached with a dull pain. To him, the pain was a constant reminder of what waited ahead.

***

"We walk to teach a lesson—your first lesson," replied Xith. Vilmos had been asking him questions ever since they crossed the river this morning and though he was growing irritated, he was pleased. Vilmos was genuinely interested in just about everything. "*The most important lesson of all*. There is *no simple path to follow*. Once you begin a course of action, you must follow it through. Beside, it would be unwise to try to teleport to our destination. You would learn nothing and would most likely—"

"Teleport?"

"Yes teleport." Xith held back a chuckle, knowing a secret yearn the boy was not aware of. "True teleportation, or moving from one place to another through magic, is very powerful magic. You must understand that. *It is a feat few magicians may attempt. To fail is to bring your own demise*. It is a special kind of incantation that draws heavily upon the threads of the universe. One must also know exactly where they are going in order to teleport."

"You don't know where we are going?"

"Yes I do, but you do not. For the spell to be successful, to teleport the two of us to where we travel, you must also know precisely the point to which we go."

"Then tell me—"

"—I am afraid it is not that simple. For now, *we will walk*," Xith said, using the Voice to end the conversation.

Xith stopped for a moment to open the leather bag that he had slung over his left shoulder. "Here, eat this."

"What is it?"

"Dried fish."

Vilmos invoked a sour face in disgust, but he was hungry. He disliked fish and decided after he swallowed the last bite that he especially disliked dried fish. Xith raised a warding hand as Vilmos started to speak again, waving his hands wildly and pointing to the ground, meaning for Vilmos to stoop low.

"What's wrong?" whispered Vilmos, not

moving.

"Shh!" responded Xith, "*Get down.*"

The response automatic, Vilmos sank low and moved to the tall grasses that grew along the river's course. For a time silence followed, then abruptly his ears filled with the cacophony of hooves. Vilmos hugged the grasses closely and clung to the ground for safety. The sound of hundreds of horses, the clash of whips and voices soon became overbearing. Vilmos had to block them out. He clasped his hands tightly to his ears and pushed vigorously until the sounds were muffled.

The ground trembled in the wake of the riders' procession and in his fright, Vilmos pushed with such force his head began to throb with pain.

"Make it stop," Vilmos whispered. The unmistakable rasping and creaking of a wagon passing in proximity to his position swelled to his ears despite the intended barrier. Wanting to run became the most prevalent thought in his mind, but would he be caught? What would they do to him if they caught him? And where was Xith?

Hesitantly, Vilmos opened his eyes and craned his head up slightly. Wagons were still passing and behind them came many more riders. Carefully Vilmos checked the area to his left and right, his hands never shifting from on top of his ears. Xith was nowhere in his eyesight and now Vilmos was really feeling frightened and alone.

The voices he heard seemed harsh and cruel, and the cracks of their whips sent shivers down his back. *Please, oh please, don't let them hurt me.*

Seconds ticked by to the pace of his heartbeats. Vilmos prayed to Great-Father to keep him safe. Eventually though the sounds grew distant and as quickly as they had appeared, the men and horses disappeared.

Before daring to crawl from the high grass cover, Vilmos waited until he could no longer hear the sounds of movement. Hesitantly he rose from his crawl to a half stoop, and stared along the trail in the direction that the sounds had retreated.

"Xith? Xith? Where are you?"

Xith's answer was calm. "Yes, Vilmos I am with you."

"Who were those men?"

"They are the reason we must travel swiftly."

With his eyes filled with fright, Vilmos asked, "Would they have killed me?"

"There are worse fates than death, Vilmos."

Vilmos brushed the grass and dirt from his clothing. "Where are they going? And why are they in the valley?"

"Most likely they use the valley for the same reason we do. It is safer than the forest."

"Why would such a large group fear the forest?"

Xith turned to stare at the trail of dust rising from the valley floor. "Why indeed."

***

Two long and uneventful days followed the encounter near the river, and on the eve of their fourth day in the valley Vilmos and Xith completed the crossing to the northern rim. Low bluffs on one side and gentle hills on the other replaced the high cliff walls of the southern rim. The two weary travelers found a small cave nestled in a low wall and they stopped to pass the night. The cave was just as dreary as Vilmos had always imagined a cave would be—damp and dark, offering nothing that appealed to his senses. He almost would have rather slept outside on the hard ground.

"Well, what are you waiting for? I am sure you will find some brush just outside that will make us a good warm fire," said Xith.

Vilmos considered another time when Xith spoke those words. It seemed now a distant memory—not altogether forgotten, but rather something that had occurred long ago. Yet now he recalled the thought fondly and smiled as he retreated from the cavern.

After a small bundle of assorted twigs and small sticks was neatly stockpiled Vilmos went in search of larger firewood and found some not far off. When Vilmos returned a second time, Xith indicated that he need gather no more wood. They would have plenty to carry them through the hours of darkness and to cook their breakfast if they so chose.

"Good," Xith said. "Set the wood in the center of the chamber and start the fire while we still have a little light from the outside."

Vilmos did as Xith stated and built the fire base. When finished, he looked to Xith, waiting for the shaman to give him something to start the fire with.

Xith rummaged through his bags for a few moments, then set them aside. "Sorry, I must have lost the flint and steel."

"Lost? How can I start a fire without it?"

"Are you always so stubborn? Use that which you have. You must always *use the tools* that you have been provided. Do not be afraid to *use your natural talents*."

Vilmos searched in the dim light until he found something he could use: two stones, which he picked up and began to strike together trying to make a spark. Xith watched enthusiastically. Vilmos had such determination that Xith almost believed Vilmos would light the fire by striking the stones together.

Several frustrating minutes later, after Vilmos had smashed his fingers a few times, he gave up. He looked to Xith for a hint of approval or some sign to stop but Xith offered no response.

Vilmos didn't want to disappoint the shaman. He snarled back a frown and returned to pounding the rocks together. Yet after smashing two more fingers, Vilmos cast the stones against the cavern wall. "I give up, I simply can't do it."

"You just aren't trying hard enough."

"What do you mean, I'm not trying hard enough?"

Xith stood and moved toward Vilmos. "I mean you're not trying hard enough."

"That's it," Vilmos said, "I've had it."

"*Calm down,*" said Xith, "listen to me closely. All right?"

Vilmos nodded.

"You are going about this in the wrong manner. I said, '*use your natural talents*'. *Magic* is one of your greatest talents, Vilmos."

"But, I don't know how to use it that way."

"*Try,*" invoked Xith. "All you have to do is try. You have the ability, *it is easy.*"

Vilmos mulled over Xith's words for a moment. Still, he was afraid of his magic. Nothing good had ever come from using it. "No, I will not do it."

"There is nothing to fear, just *listen* to me. Draw the energy into you, but slowly. Only *build the power* that you need," instructed Xith, watching the boy's face carefully. "*Can you feel it?*"

Vilmos did as told. He drew the power in slowly. "I can feel it!" he exclaimed, "I can feel it!"

"Good, now *focus* on the *fire* and turn the energy inside you onto it."

"H-how do I do that?" Vilmos was confused.

"Do not think about the how," said Xith, "just do. *Focus* the energy on the fire, think about lighting it."

Vilmos thought, enough already, I'll do it. A minute spark lit the room for an instant. Vilmos started, and then became frustrated. "I can't!"

"You mean you won't do it. You block the energy flow. You must *think positive*. You must *know you can do* something simply because you can.

Do not worry that you won't be able to do it. Follow my instructions closely. *Are you ready, Vilmos?*"

Vilmos shrugged.

"Take a deep breath. *Breathe* it in slowly."

Vilmos inhaled a deep breath as Xith had instructed, his lungs filled with air.

"Feel the air inside your lungs," Xith said. "Feel it fill them *full*."

Vilmos did.

"Now exhale, continue to breathe deeply, feel the air flow in and out. *Feel* the *life* within you."

Vilmos did as he was instructed.

"Continue to breathe, clear your mind." Xith's eyes glowed. More stirred within the boy than magic alone.

"I'm trying—"

"—Shh… *Listen*," commanded Xith. He smiled. "Clear your mind. *Concentrate* only on breathing."

Vilmos cleared his mind until his only thoughts were of his breathing.

"*Focus* the energy. *Concentrate*. *Gather* it in slowly."

Xith waited. Vilmos brought the power in slowly as instructed.

"Find your center. *Draw upon the power* around you, drink it in—but only a small amount. Focus the energy. *Use it now*."

Vilmos did as Xith stated. The energy was there and, thankfully, he was able to focus it. Suddenly a brilliant, blue–white flame burst amidst the wood.

"Wow, I did it!" Vilmos exclaimed, eyes wide with amazement.

"Yes, but next time try not to waste so much energy."

Missing the false sarcasm in Xith's voice, Vilmos elected to ignore Xith's comment and enjoy the fire. It was, after all, warm, and did offer some cheer to the otherwise dank cavern. He removed his boots and placed them next to the fire, stretching out his short, stubby toes to the warm blaze to soothe his blistered feet.

Xith opened his pack and pulled out some foodstuffs, splitting the last of the supply of bread and cheese between the two of them, offering the largest share to Vilmos.

"Eat hearty, Vilmos, and then get some sleep. You will need a good rest, for tomorrow will be a long day."

The day's trek had left Vilmos ravenous and he attacked the food vigorously. He was always hungry. Eating was almost his favorite pastime. Within minutes, he had gobbled down his share and was staring intently toward Xith's, which the shaman had barely nibbled at.

"Go ahead, Vilmos, take it. You are a growing boy. Eat."

Vilmos raised his eyebrows. Are you sure? His expression read. Xith nodded.

***

Vilmos' mind was teaming with questions, so many that he didn't know which to ask first. He considered them one at a time, and then selected the one he deemed to be the most important. "Xith, will you tell me NOW where we travel to?"

"Get some *rest*," replied Xith, "tomorrow is another day."

Vilmos leaned back and patted an excessively full belly. "Then tell me about your people. What are they like?"

"*Sleep*, Vilmos."

"But Xith, I'm not really tired."

Xith eyed Vilmos. "Yes, you are, now *sleep*."

Xith waited, interested in the response and the apparent rejection of the guile's of Voice.

"But—"

"—No more questions, go to *sleep*!" yelled Xith.

Vilmos stretched out next to the fire and with eyes almost closed, he feigned sleep. Bodily tired but with a mind too full of unanswered questions to sleep, he eventually turned frank eyes cautiously to the place where Xith sat, eyes wide, feet stretched out, hands happily stroking a long wooden stick, whittling it away with a short tooling knife.

"Xith?" Vilmos called out with a hint of boldness.

"Save your strength, you will need it," said Xith, not looking up. "Tomorrow will be a long day in Vangar Forest."

Vilmos sat up, his eyes filled with sincerity. "But why was it safe to use the magic now and not before? Are the dreams gone? And why did Midori have to go? And why—"

"—Shh," Xith said. Xith set aside his knife and stick, and then waved a hand over the fire. The flames sprang back, seemingly into the wood, until only a few tiny flames remained.

"A great many things will be explained at a time when I know you are ready to hear them. Too much awaits in the days ahead for me to properly begin your education. You have chosen to accept the way of the Magus as your way of life, and, as such, you must know that nothing is ever simply revealed all at once, rather in bits and pieces.

"Your use of magic alone didn't bring me to you, it was also your dreams. Once I sensed them, I sent Midori to watch over you until it was time. When the time was near, I came."

Xith waved his hand over the fire again. The flames turned white. Vilmos saw images playing amidst them. He leaned forward, his eyebrows knotted together as at first he became confused then alarmed.

"Pieces of your dreams," Xith said. "All those who have special gifts are troubled by such dreams. They are the playing out of good and evil. They are the reason magic is forbidden, for during the dismal centuries before and after the Race Wars, the unwary so easily succumbed to the destructive nature of dark magic that in the end it became more prudent to destroy would-be mages than to try to save them from themselves.

"The Watchers were born of this period, and we took it upon ourselves to save those we could, for we knew what peril lay in a world without magic." Xith's tone became melancholy. "That I am the last of the Watchers there is little doubt, and when I breathe my last breath, there will be no more watch wardens and magic will surely fade from the land."

Xith picked up the staff he had been working on, and then he reached back into his pack and pulled out another. Even in the pale light Vilmos could see that the second staff was the one Xith normally used.

"But in the interim, I do what I can, and what I must." Xith moved the staff he had been whittling toward Vilmos but didn't let him touch it. "When I finish this, I will give it to you. And on that day you will know that your education is truly beginning."

Vilmos grinned, then frowned. "But what of the dreams, are they gone?"

Xith put the staffs away. He regarded Vilmos for a time, then said, "To any other, I would say yes. To you, I say we will have to wait and see."

Chapters 9 and 10: Review Questions

1. Why does Seth decide to rely on Captain Cagan when the elves are ambushed?

2. What does it mean to guide a ship into the head of a gull, and why did Cagan do that?

3. Why does Cagan say, "It is only us at the last."?

4. How does Vilmos discover he won't be going home? Would you trust Xith like Vilmos does?

5. What happens when Vilmos learns that his "father" really loved him?

6. Where is Xith taking Vilmos, and what hints does Vilmos give that his perception about this place is different than Xith's or others who may live in this place?

7. What do you think Xith means when he says, "There is no simple path to follow," and what is he trying to teach Vilmos?

8. What does Xith reveal about magic and Vilmos' dreams?

Words to Watch

Traversable	Preoccupy	Aggravate
Infrequent	Recuperate	Tributary
Independent	Awareness	Detachment
Peddler	Extensive	Sheepishly
Holding (N.)	Company	Dilapidated
Fortunate	Column	Complement
Commander	Whinny	

Chapter Eleven: Decision

The plains beyond Imtal Palace, the rolling foothills of the Braddabaggon and the green of the forest were all far behind Adrina now. The day before they had passed through the quiet village Captain Brodst had been trying to reach the night of the heavy rains—the night Adrina had met the mysterious lady in the forest. Early this morning the column had crossed into Mellack proper.

The new day surprisingly brought a beautiful, clear sky. Adrina's mood became quite cheerful despite her saddle sore backside and her heavy thoughts. The southern road, though still muddied, was readily traversable and the column was able to travel at a remarkably good pace considering their rate the previous days. Adrina had seen very few passers by this day—only a few merchants which Captain Brodst had sent immediately away to peddle their wares elsewhere, and the infrequent travelers who hurried along on independent missions.

Over the past day and a half, Adrina had thought of little else other than the words of the mysterious lady and the heir to the throne of Sever—Prince William. She had only met the young prince once, but that had been three long years ago at her mother's funeral. She remembered little of her distant cousin, only that he had the bluest eyes she'd ever seen.

Adrina watched everything and everyone she passed—thinking every pair of peddlers would be the two strangers or that every guardsman that came near her was the traitor. "You must open your eyes," the lady had told her, and Adrina had.

Emel had stayed as close to Adrina as his duties allowed. The two had discussed several plans of action but nothing they came up with seemed appropriate. The lady had told them to tell no one of their conversation, but how could they do otherwise? They had to tell someone—for how could they stop the column from proceeding onward to Alderan. But who?

A sounding of the horns signaled a slackening of the pace, and as Adrina looked up she saw Emel racing back to the middle of the column. Two hours ago he had been sent out to lead a scouting party.

Adrina nodded her head as he passed her. She noticed he looked nervous and knew he would return as soon as he reported the group's findings. Captain Brodst had been sending out scouting parties at regular intervals ever since they had crossed into Mellack Proper. Adrina guessed that this was because Mellack Proper was a king's holding without a garrison. The citizens of Mellack looked to the Duchy of Ispeth that bordered it to the southeast and to Imtal to the north for its defense.

She didn't have to wait long though. Emel was reining Ebony Lightning in beside her a few minutes later.

"Did you see something?" she excitedly asked him.

"I wish," Emel replied. "Nothing but fields as far as the eye can see."

"Why are you sweating so? You look peaked. What is wrong?"

Emel smiled devilishly. "Ebony wanted to race, so I pressed the group hard. I saw no harm in it. We are nearly upon the borders of Ispeth now."

"Isn't much to Mellack Proper, is there?"

The expression on Emel's face grew grim. He lowered his voice to a whisper as he began to speak. "Did you know that tomorrow a detachment will break from the main company?"

Adrina turned frank eyes upon Emel. "Have you thought of what I said earlier?"

"I've thought of little else." There was evident tension in Emel's voice. "Do you really think it is wise?"

"Do we have any other choice? The way I see it we have to talk to someone about this and who better than Father Jacob, Keeper Martin or Captain Brodst."

"Why do I have to be the one who makes the choice of which to talk to?"

Adrina said nothing in reply.

"I never should have turned back," muttered Emel, thinking Adrina couldn't hear him, but she did. She winked at him.

"I'm glad you did," admitted Adrina. "I couldn't have shouldered this alone. You are a true friend."

"This is not a choice I want to make hastily." Ebony nickered. Emel stroked the stallion's mane. "I need more time. Besides, my father wants me at the fore of the column. We can talk again later. Agreed?"

Concern in her eyes, Adrina watched Emel ride off. Afterward her thoughts turned back to the road. An afternoon sun was just starting its descent and passing clouds brought dark shadows to the land. She hoped it wouldn't rain again and as time passed and rain did not come, she counted herself fortunate.

She listened to the clatter-clatter of hooves and heels along the hardening ground. The company had returned to a four-abreast formation with one squadron of garrison soldiers to the fore of her position and two to the rear. The palace guardsmen and the distinguished guests made up the middle of the formation with protective files set up along both sides of them.

Great Kingdom had few bandits in its heartland but Adrina knew Captain Brodst thought one could never be overcautious. As she looked on, the captain surveyed his group from end to end. He was conferring with the three commanders. From his especially grave scowl Adrina guessed it wasn't pleasant words he spoke to them. Of the three, Captain Adylton, Captain Ghenson and Captain Trendmore, it was only Captain Trendmore that she thought warranted closer attention. Trendmore was an ambitious and manipulative man, or so Adrina had once heard during a session of her father's court.

Adrina chased after Emel in her thoughts now and, preoccupied with this, she had not taken notice of the keeper's presence beside her nor had she heard his words of inquiry until he spoke louder. She started at the voice, jumped in the saddle and then had to rein in her mount to curb its excitement which matched her own.

"What troubles the mind of one so young and beautiful?" asked Keeper Martin.

Recovering her senses, Adrina said, "Beautiful day, keeper."

Martin mumbled something inaudible.

"Have you decided if you will continue to

Alderan with us or not keeper?"

"The East–West crossroads are but a day away. I may yet change my mind and go south with the party to Quashan', dear." Gray-haired Martin paused. "In truth, I am awaiting response to the message I sent to Keeper Q'yer. If all goes well I should receive it this night."

"Tonight?"

"Keeper Q'yer has had his week to recuperate from the last sending."

Adrina turned frank eyes on the keeper. "A dream message?"

The keeper smiled knowingly, but didn't say anything immediately. Adrina knew little about the mysterious Lore Keepers, who in recent years had detached themselves from palace proceedings yet still seemed to know everything that went on in Imtal. She knew the keeper to be a man who preferred his records and his tomes to human companionship—at least that is what she had heard.

"You have careful ears dear. Where did you hear such a thing?" asked Keeper Martin—a check for honesty, among his other duties as Head Keeper was to track the history of the royal family. At the age of consent, it would be time to draft a new tome, one with the young princess' name inscribed upon its leather binding.

"Why, from your own lips keeper."

"A dream message is a form of communication," said Martin, his words sounding like an oration, "a keeper can deliver a message to another keeper in the form of a message that enters their awareness and takes the form of a dream."

"But how is such a thing possible?"

"Actually, very simply. The real difficulty lies in the proper use of your will. To begin you must clear all thoughts from your mind and reach into the center of your being. A spark of power lies there that is your soul. You reach out with that power until you touch the consciousness of the one you wish to communicate with. You speak through images and feelings that you create in your consciousness and pass... Boring you dear? I am sorry, I tend to babble."

Adrina tried to remain focused on her goal, which was to find out what the keeper knew of their destination, but she was caught in the interest of the ideas he presented to her and this perplexed her. "No, Keeper Martin, you're not boring me. Can anyone do this? How come you can't use words?"

"Slow down dear," said the keeper with equal enthusiasm. "Only a few know how to properly utilize their conscious to create the message. It is part of the knowledge passed down from Great-Father to us alone, the Keepers of the Lore. Throughout time there have been others who learned to use this power. Unfortunately, though, only the keepers retain this skill now."

"But I don't understand. How can you comprehend the dream if you do not use words?"

"I did not say that words could not be used." Martin paused, adding extra meaning to the statement. "It takes an extremely powerful center to create a vision in the form of thoughts that enter another's awareness as audible words. The simpler form is to use images and feelings."

"Keeper can you teach me, I mean... can you teach me how to use the dream message?" Adrina was excited now and did little to hide it.

"I can teach you the theory." The keeper sighed with lament. "But I am afraid it is a moot undertaking."

Adrina thought about his words for a moment. She still wanted to know what he knew about their destination but she *was* genuinely intrigued. She also hoped this would give her a chance to talk to the keeper alone. She had made her choice, she would tell the keeper of her troubles. She had only to tell Emel this now. "I do not mind. There is nothing better to do with my time at present—if you do not mind imparting your wisdom to me, of course?"

The keeper's eyes gleamed as he said, "Of course I don't mind. In fact, I'll take great pleasure in it. We'll start this evening."

***

Captain Brodst called the column to a halt near the borders of Ispeth. "Eat well and rest your feet and your mounts," he advised. "If the good weather holds we will try to make up the distance we lost to rains the days before. The earlier we reach the crossroads tomorrow, the better."

Adrina eagerly dismounted and followed Father Jacob and Keeper Martin to the top of a small rise where the commanders and the guests would have their midday meal. Mostly she wanted to listen in on their conversations, but she was also very hungry.

From atop the hill she could look down on the whole of the extensive company. Ridesmen were tending to their mounts. Foot soldiers were resting tired feet. Obviously unhappy guards were posted fore and aft.

Not far off Adrina saw Emel and the small band of young ridesmen—twelve in all—that had survived the encounter with the lowland cat of the Braddabaggon. Little of their conversation rose to her ears, but she could tell the foul weather hadn't dampened their high spirits. To them, the journey to Alderan was still high adventure. Adrina wasn't so sure anymore, though she still longed to feel hot sands between her toes and taste the salty spray of wind-blown seas.

True to his word, Emel found Adrina shortly after Captain Brodst called the column to movement. But before she could say anything of her conversation with Keeper Martin, Emel spoke his mind. "I have given it much thought," he said furrowing his eyebrows and borrowing his father's scowl, "I truly do not know Father Jacob or Keeper Martin. I am sure they are both men of honor but I cannot vouch for their word. My father, the captain, on the other hand is a man who lives by his sense of honor and I can vouch for his word. He has never knowingly broken a trust."

Adrina didn't know what to say. She had tried to interrupt Emel but he hadn't let her. Just as she was about to say something, her mare whinnied. For some reason the horse liked her to run her hands along its withers and the base of the mane and scratch. She also thought the mare was fond of Emel's Ebony.

"There, there girl," she whispered to calm the animal. Then turning to Emel she said, "What of Keeper Martin? He is by far the wisest man in the kingdom."

"See, there you go. I make a choice and you don't like it."

Adrina was quick to explain about her earlier conversation with the keeper. "So you see," she concluded, "isn't Keeper Martin the best choice?"

"But when will we ever get him alone? He's never alone."

"This evening. He promised to talk to me. We'll find a quiet place to converse and you'll join us."

Emel signaled agreement and for a time afterward no words passed between them.

It was not long before the company crossed into the Duchy of Ispeth. The quiet fields of Mellack Proper were left behind and now groves of fruit trees lined the road. The apples of Duke Ispeth were the best in the land and often graced the king's table.

It was nearly autumn. Many of the trees were laden with fruit. The sweet scent of apples, heavy in the air, was mouth watering. Adrina saw more than a few soldiers climbing trees and filling bags—no doubt they were claiming the apples in the name of King Andrew.

Barely an hour after crossing into the Duchy of Ispeth, a vanguard of the Duke's small army was already on its way toward them. Adrina watched Emel and the riders around her grow agitated at the show of force. She didn't know why, because the soldiers of the column outnumbered the small group of Ispeth knights a hundred to one.

Captain Brodst commanded the column to a halt and saying, "Stand at ease. Two runners. Banners high. Forward," dispatched messengers carrying the king's banner to greet the approaching riders.

"There's Duke Ispeth himself," said Emel unhappily.

Adrina maneuvered her mare closer to Emel. "You've met him?"

"I *was* a king's messenger. Crossing into Ispeth uninvited isn't wise."

Emel made no further comment on the matter even when Adrina pressed him. She imagined that he'd met the duke before. She'd heard about the eccentric duke and seen him on several occasions, though he rarely attended the king's court.

"What are they doing now?" Adrina asked. "Are they setting up a tent?"

Emel didn't need to respond. The duke had apparently ordered that two tents be built and workers were busily staking out the lines for the canvas. After the tents were erected, Duke Ispeth and Captain Brodst met in conference. Keeper Martin, Father Jacob and the three commanders were summarily summoned.

"What's going on?" asked Adrina.

"Duke Ispeth is not the most trusting of men. I've had the pleasure of his company on several occasions, I know. If he sees plots and spies in the passage of a mere messenger across Ispeth who knows what he thinks seeing this mob… We'll not be traveling any more this day."

"At least we may get the chance to talk to Keeper Martin earlier than we planned…"

***

Long after Adrina had bedded down the previous night, Captain Brodst and the others had been in Duke Ispeth's tent. What they had talked about during those many hours Adrina didn't know, she only knew her hopes of talking to Keeper Martin had faded hour by hour.

"Emel," called out Adrina, flagging him down with her hands as he rode past. She attempted to make conversation with him as she had tried earlier. Again he cut her off and rode on ahead. It didn't seem intentional, though, because he seemed worried about something. She thought it possibly related to the conversation the captain had had with the *acting* sergeant before they broke camp. She hadn't been able to discern their whispers but the conversation had seemed rather one-sided, with Emel doing most of the listening.

Aggravated she wrapped the reins tight in her hands and spurred her mare on. "Oh no you don't, Emel Brodstson!" she screamed after him.

Emel reined Ebony in and wheeled about to face Adrina. He didn't say a word. He didn't need to. His stare was angry and cold.

"Did I do something?" asked Adrina near tears.

Emel cast a glum stare toward the rear of the column. Adrina could only guess that it was directed at the captain. "I am sorry, Adrina," he said, turning away and chiding Ebony into movement, "I tried, I really did."

Adrina brought her mare along side Emel's Ebony. "Slow down, talk to me."

"My group has forward position throughout the morning."

"Is that all that's wrong? You don't have to protect me at all times. I saw you relieve the central guard again last night. You can't keep standing watch all night and riding all day. You'll drop out of the saddle."

"The Duchy of Ispeth is not all sweet-smelling orchards you know. At one time, this was swamp as far as the eye could see. That is, before Ispeth River and its tributaries dried up, or so it is said. The farther south you go, the wetter the climate becomes. In a few days, you'll reach the swamps and if you're lucky the company will skirt them, if you're not you'll take the Kingdom road through them.

"Since you have to keep pace with the column, it'll take you a week to skirt the swamp. Or at the very least three days by the King's road. Ebony and I cut through the Bottoms *once*. There are things in there without names, but they'll try to take you just the same. They don't call it the bottom of the world for nothing.

"Fog rolls in so thick by mid-afternoon that you can't see your hand in front of your face. I dropped my torch, *my torch*, and nearly lost it. It was the longest twelve hours alone of my life. I nearly lost my wits. It's a good thing Ebony was with me. Just before sunrise we went in, and an hour past sunset we came out."

"There's nothing that will get me," said Adrina. A proud smile came to her lips. "I have Emel Brodstson to guard me."

Emel's next words were drowned out by the sounds of the column.

Adrina shrugged. "I can't hear you."

"I am to go south with the detachment to Quashan'," said Emel, in a soft, sorrowful voice. Afterward he spurred Ebony on and didn't look back.

Adrina returned to her place in the column. A dull pain in the pit of her stomach told her of emotions she sought to hold in. No tears ran down her cheeks, though several times she fought them back as they welled up in her eyes. Emel was the only one who shared her secret.

Anger and disillusionment found her. Hadn't the lady in the forest said Emel was now a part of that secret? Didn't that mean he should remain with her at least until they decided what to do? They hadn't decided anything, except to talk to Keeper Martin, which they hadn't been able to do.

She listened to the sound of hooves and heels for a long time afterward. Only the far off angry calls of birds from amidst the apple orchards aroused her to the world—apple pickers were chasing the birds from the trees.

As she turned to watch a flock of black birds rise from the trees, Adrina caught sight of Keeper Martin and Father Jacob returning from the rear of the column. Suddenly resolved to talk to the keeper, she slowed her mare and allowed them to overtake her. Determination in her eye, she said, "Beautiful day, Keeper Martin, Father Jacob. Keeper, what news of the dream message? We will reach the crossroads in a few hours."

Gray-haired Martin grinned sheepishly. "I did not hold to my word did I, Young Highness. I am truly sorry. Duke Ispeth is both persistent and long-winded. He would have rambled on and on through the night if Captain Brodst hadn't put an end to it when he did. And yes, Keeper Q'yer's message arrived."

Adrina flashed her eyes at the keeper. Well? They asked.

"Indeed," said Martin, tugging on his unkempt beard and turning to Father Jacob.

Jacob who had been nibbling on an apple cast the core away. Adrina caught sight of the great swirling white circles that decorated the sleeves of his otherwise black robe. The circles that had once been bright white were now dull and dirty, coated with the dust of the road.

"I have given it much thought," said the priest, pausing to sigh. "You are right. I can sense it too. It is all around us."

"Then you have considered what we discussed?" asked Keeper Martin.

"I have, but I do not think this is the right time to discuss this."

"Indeed," said Martin, scratching at his beard again.

Adrina didn't say a word. She hoped the two would forget she was even there.

"Please forgive us, dear," said Martin turning to her. "Our thoughts are on other things at the moment. Perhaps it would be best if we talked later."

"Then you will be continuing with us?"

The Lore Keeper turned to Father Jacob then said, "Yes, I believe I will."

***

The column reached the East–West Road late in the day and here they stopped. The great road stood barren before them, its wide span thick with mud and seemingly sullen. There had been a settlement here once but all that remained were dilapidated and decaying buildings.

West along the sea lay the Barony of Klaive, across the swamps to the great sea lay the Twin Sonnets, the Free Cities of Mir and Veter. East, a long, long way along the great road lay the end of Great Kingdom and the beginning of the Western Territories. Here the land was shrouded in ancient woodlands, a forest as deep and rich as the whole of the Territories, Eastern and Western. Directly to their south lay South Province and its capital Quashan'. To the north, Imtal awaited their return.

From here, a small complement of ridesmen, two detachments and the acting sergeant at arms, Emel Brodstson, would continue south. The remainder of the great company would follow the gradual westward slope of the road for a few more hours.

Adrina watched as the detachment rode away to the south and she rode westward. Decidedly, she would miss Emel. She wanted to chase him down and wish him a safe journey or maybe mumble through an apology, but held back.

She would have continued riding west and never spoken the good-bye she was harboring if a few moments of hesitation hadn't changed her mind—she did want to chase after him. She wrapped the leather straps tightly in her hands and pulled them sharply to one side to turn the mare quickly. A swift kick to the hindquarters sent the mount charging.

Not quite sure what she wanted to tell him, she was slow to call out to him.

"Emel, Emel!" she yelled.

She wanted to tell him that it wasn't his fault. She wanted to tell him what she felt for him in her heart. She wanted to tell him that she would miss him. Yet as he turned to look at her, she found her tongue growing limp.

"Please give my regards to Prince Valam. Tell my brother I can't wait until his visit next summer," she said, saying what was safe and not what was in her heart.

Emel returned a pithy, acknowledging smile.

Chapter 11: Word Jumble

Traversable Preoccupy Aggravate
Infrequent Recuperate Tributary
Independent Awareness Detachment
Peddler Extensive Sheepishly
Holding (N.) Company Dilapidated
Fortunate Column Complement
Commander Whinny

Word jumble: Unjumble the letters of these vocabulary words. Hint: Column 1.

Qetnfneuri
Pdtneeenind
Mdnrcoame
Ldreepd
Lbaresavrte
Entroauft
Dglniho

Word jumble: Unjumble the letters of these vocabulary words. Hint: Column 2.

Txvieseen
Sneraawse
Rteapcueer
Npycmoa
Nhywni
Lnmouc
Cuoppcrey

Word jumble: Unjumble the letters of these vocabulary words. Hint: Column 3.

Ubritrtya
Atevargga
Pdtldiidaea
Lpeetnocmm
Hsyleephsi
Hcanemdett

Words to Watch

Sprawling	Boundless
Brambles	Glistening
Gradually	Objective
Progress	Staggered
Interval	Saturated
Overwhelming	Infection
Rationalize	Terrifying

Chapter Twelve: Vangar Forest

Three hours after dawn they entered the forest. Almost immediately, Vilmos felt the crawl of unseen eyes upon him, but he did not really start to worry until the sun disappeared, blocked out by the forest canopy.

Despite ever thickening undergrowth, Xith maintained a steady pace, trying to stay directed north. At times it seemed as if the forest had a will of its own. Sprawling rows of brambles seemed to close any gaps as they approached and the two would have to travel either west or east until they finally chanced upon a break. Sometimes this distance was only a hundred yards. But more than once, it seemed as if the brambles had stretched on for miles.

"Stay close," Xith advised for the second time.

"I still don't understand why we didn't use the road the soldiers cut through the forest," complained Vilmos. "Surely it went directly north."

"*Silence*," commanded Xith.

Vilmos turned as the shaman had and saw movement out of the corner of his eye. His heart started pounding in his ears and a lump swelled up in his throat.

"*Run*," shouted Xith, pushing Vilmos. "No matter what happens do not look back. Do you understand?"

Vilmos said nothing. Xith twisted him around and stared into his eyes. "Do you understand?"

Vilmos nodded.

The two ran in a flat out race. Trees became black blurs. They no longer turned at brambles; instead they plowed through them with Xith pushing Vilmos ever forward.

Cuts and scrapes on his hands, face and arms, bruises on his knees, Vilmos ran on. He ran as fast as he could. Every now and again he saw black shapes out of the corner of his eye that he was certain were not trees. But it was only when he heard the first tormented howl that he became certain he was running for his very life.

Soon the tormented cries of the unknown beasts came from many directions then gradually the howls grew closer and closer. Xith pushed Vilmos faster and faster, surprising the boy with his seemingly endless endurance.

Nervously, Vilmos glanced to his left and to the rear. His feet lead him to the right—there were no cries coming from the right. Then suddenly the shaman stopped and Vilmos only heard the sound of his own running. He stopped then, turned around, ran back to where the Shaman stood. His eyes grew wide with terror and his heart pounded so loudly in his ears that he couldn't hear what the shaman was saying. He only knew the shaman was staring into the shadows of the forest.

"They are leading us," Xith said, "do not let your feet stray."

The two started running again. Terror helped

Vilmos find his second wind and soon he was outpacing Xith.

Coming down a ravine, Vilmos stumbled and fell. Xith picked him up by the scruff of his collar and lead him on. They breached a hill, crossed a stream, ran on in soggy shoes, on and on they raced.

Vilmos was running to the pace of his heart, which was still pounding in his ears. He stretched his small body to its limits, again surprised at the shaman's seemingly boundless stamina. More than once he doubled over in pain and fought to catch his breath, and more than once the shaman forced him into movement. Sometimes dragging him by the arm or the collar. Sometimes pushing him. Sometimes just his wild stare was enough to force Vilmos to find his next wind.

Then suddenly they burst into a clearing. A midday sun shining overhead told Vilmos they were safe, they were out of the dark forest. A sigh of relief escaped his lips.

Then just as Vilmos paused to catch his breath, Xith directed his gaze to the other side of the clearing. The forest stretched on endlessly, the trunks of trees fading into the gloomy shadows.

Vilmos tried desperately to catch his breath. "Can we rest, please?"

"Not long," cautioned Xith, "those beasts aren't far behind us."

"What are they?"

"Some things are best left unnamed. To be sure, their masters are the reason the animals of the forest are angry." Xith's eyes darted to the shadows. "Run now, run as if your life depends on it, because it does."

"I need... more rest," said Vilmos, panting, "can you not use your magic on them?"

"For every one I sent back to the pits where they spawned, two more would come. No, we *run*," said Xith, launching Vilmos into a run by pushing him forcefully with both hands.

***

Vilmos stumbled, fell, came up on his feet again. For a moment in his confusion, he thought Xith wasn't with him anymore, but then he caught a glimpse of the shaman's brown robe. Exhausted, Vilmos no longer ran. He simply plodded along, forcing himself to put one foot in front of the other, required great effort.

Time progressed slowly. Most of the tormented howls faded to distant echoes and now it seemed only one of the strange beasts followed them. Vilmos heard its high-pitched howl sound off to his left.

By now they had gone so far and so deep into the forest and strayed off course so many times that Vilmos thought surely even the shaman had lost his way long ago. The beasts *were* leading them, forcing them to take an increasingly easterly course.

Vilmos could no longer determine shapes in the shadows. Everything was shadows and dull grays slowly turned black. Night was surely near.

The touch of a hand to his shoulder caused Vilmos to start. He jumped and nearly screamed. Xith whispered in a low voice, "Tie this rope around your waist. It will keep us from being separated."

Vilmos took the offered rope and began tying it about his waist.

"Follow where I lead you," said Xith. "Keep your hands out in front of your face protectively."

Vilmos finished securing the rope. He caught sight of a soft glow from the shaman's eyes. They were glistening silver once more. "Do your eyes allow you to see in the dark?"

Xith grinned. "It is the gift of Oread to her people."

Vilmos stretched his sore muscles, and eased the fire away from aching legs, then finally asked the question that had been bothering him for what seemed hours. "Are we lost?"

"The sense of direction of the peoples of Under-Earth is keen. Do not worry my young friend. Soon we will leave the Forest of Vangar and all of this will be behind us for a time."

Xith said nothing more, except that they should begin moving again.

**

Vilmos followed where the pull of the rope lead him, the world around him was now so black that he couldn't discern anything from the darkness that surrounded him. Not knowing when they would come to a rut, a hill, a ravine, he placed each foot down softly and uncertainly. He tried to keep his thoughts from wandering and think only of placing one foot in front of the other. This was a difficult chore as he fought exhaustion.

The single hunter continued to follow them, howling out at seemingly regular intervals—perhaps telling companions that followed silently that the hunt was still on.

Staring into the darkness and not being able to see anything was at times overwhelming and during those times, Vilmos felt utterly helpless. He could only follow the tugs at the rope and hope that the person tied to the other end was still Xith—for exhaustion made him doubt even that.

His thoughts did wander though, even as he fought to keep them focused on putting one foot in front of the other. He thought of home, the villagers, and Lillath and Vil. Surely if the powerful shaman feared the creatures that chased them, the three villages were in danger. Yes, days of forests separated them, but how far did these creatures roam?

Vilmos answered the question for himself. Far enough to chase a great black bear south. Far enough to make it attack and kill the girl from Olex Village.

He groped his way around a tree that seemed to suddenly sprout in front of him. The ground beneath his feet was now damp. Vilmos knew this because of the thick mud clinging to his boots, making heavy feet that much heavier. Far off he heard the sound of running water as if a stream lay somewhere ahead. For a time his thoughts filled with a longing to drink of its cool waters.

They were coming down a long, long hill when suddenly the rope went slack. Vilmos' mind filled with alarm. Xith normally signaled with a double pull on the rope when he was going to stop.

Vilmos groped with his hands about his waist until he found where the knot in the rope began. Then he began to take up the slack in the line. When he had pulled in about five feet without the line going taut, he stopped. He was almost afraid to keep pulling. His hands way ahead of his thoughts kept working though and Vilmos soon found the end of the line in his hands.

Vilmos tried to rationalize. He told himself Xith must have untied the rope from around his waist. Perhaps the stream was just ahead and Xith wanted to tell him this. The running water did sound awfully close.

Bravely, Vilmos took a step forward into the darkness, then another, and a few more. The stream was there all right. He found it by stepping into it with a slosh—the water *was* cold.

"X-Xith," Vilmos whispered, "where are you?"

No answer.

Vilmos whispered in a slightly louder voice, "X-Xith?"

Vilmos heard movement behind him and spun about, nearly losing his balance. He saw the dull glow of a pair of eyes about halfway up the steep, forest-covered hill—but the glow wasn't soft silver.

He stood deadly still. He heard growling now and then a howl, joined by many more. Confusion, exhaustion and panic mandated his actions. Instinct and human nature took over his thoughts. The will to survive became his only objective. Blue sparks danced across his fingers tips without him even realizing it.

The light only served to fill in the images missing from his mind's eye. Halfway up the hill he saw them, a pack of the creatures that though they looked like wolves he knew they weren't. No wolf he'd even seen had two heads. No wolf he'd ever seen was as large as a bear.

Vilmos slowly backed into the stream. The creatures inched forward. He inched backward. When the waters swirling around him were knee deep, Vilmos stopped. The lead creature, the largest one of the whole pack, stood no further than ten feet away from him now. Vilmos was suddenly sure this was the beast that had hunted and howled after them while the others in the pack had hunted silently at its side. It seemed to signal to the others to wait as it approached.

Instinct and the will to survive still at the forefront of his thoughts, blue sparks continued to dance across Vilmos' fingers. He waited, staring down the strange two-headed creature, wondering why it did not attack him, wondering if it could lunge ten feet in a single, swift move using the powerful legs he saw.

Vilmos began to back up again, and the creature continued to approach. Each took one small step at a time, and stared the other down. Vilmos' two eyes matched against the creature's four, each daring the other to make a move.

The water about his legs was now only ankle deep but Vilmos gave it little thought. He dared not waver his eyes from the position they held locked to the creature's. Soon Vilmos found that he was no longer sloshing backward through water. He had come to the far bank. The strange beast waited on the opposite bank, only a few precious feet away.

In the soft blue light, the creature's double set of fangs glistened white-blue. Two heads meant two mouths filled with up-turned and down-turned canine fangs. Vilmos and the creature stared each other down, seemingly to find out whose will power was stronger.

Something brushed against his shoulder. Vilmos let out a scream that echoed long into the night. He whirled about, fists poised ready to fend off the unseen attacker, only to find soft gray eyes fixed on his.

"Xith!" Vilmos shrieked, "Thank the Father!"

"Do not thank him yet," Xith said, "back up slowly now. The Wolmerrelle will not normally leave such a place, but let's not give them any reason to think they should."

"W-Wolmerrelle?"

"Suffice it to say that species from different realms were not meant to mate, for when they do, the result is not for the greater good."

"Where did you go?" Vilmos asked as he inched backward.

Xith held out something in his hand that the boy didn't dare to look at. "They were leading us all right. Another pack was shadowing us, waiting until they had us cornered."

Xith put a heavy hand on Vilmos' shoulder, indicating they should stop. Vilmos noticed there were no trees around them. He stood in tall grass that stretched to his chest. The lead Wolmerrelle was still staring them down, but now it was a good twenty to thirty feet away. Vilmos groaned and put his hands to his face to rub bleary eyes. As Vilmos did this, Xith lost the support he had been using to keep upright. He staggered and fell.

Vilmos grabbed Xith's waist to help the

shaman to his feet. He felt moisture against his hand. Xith's robe was saturated from his neck down.

"Don't worry." Xith's voice was weak. He coughed. "Most isn't mine."

Vilmos knew then that it was blood he touched. For a moment, a small sliver of the moon shined down upon them as it broke through heavy clouds. Vilmos saw the shaman's prize. It was a head of one of the beasts; up close it was far larger and even more frightening than he had imagined.

Vilmos tended to Xith's wounds. He did as the shaman instructed and cleaned the wounds against infection then touched the stones of the river to them. "The stream is a tributary to the distant river Trollbridge that divides the Free Cities of Mir and Veter. It runs a long way from Rain Mountain in the center of the forest to where it joins the Trollbridge and helps feed the swamps. Its stones are healing in their own way," Xith had said, and Vilmos did not question that they were.

For the next several hours, Vilmos lay at Xith's side, afraid to let sleep take him. Several times as he stared through gaps in the tall grasses to the far side of the stream, Vilmos saw the strange creatures Xith had called Wolmerrelle. Xith had been right about one thing; they were best left unnamed. Putting a name to the horror he saw only aided their terrifying grip on his mind. Somehow he was sure that one day he would return to Vangar Forest and when he did, the Wolmerrelle would be waiting for him.

Next time Vilmos knew he would not be so lucky. He would not escape as easily.

Chapters 11 and 12: Review Questions

1. What decision is weighing heavily on Adrina's thoughts as she rides through Mellack Proper?

2. Who does Adrina decide to tell about her secret and why?

3. What does Adrina mean when she thinks that Keeper Martin is "a man who preferred his records and his tomes to human companionship." Do you know anyone like this?

4. Why does Emel avoid Adrina after they make camp in Ispeth?

5. Why do you think Adrina chases after Emel when he goes away, but then tells him to give her regards to her brother?

6. What happens when Vilmos and Xith enter Vangar Forest?

7. Why do you think the author calls these creatures Wolmerrelle, and what do you know about them?

8. What do you think will happen to Vilmos if he returns to Vangar Forest?

Words to Watch

Customary	Coordinated
Mire	Sentinel
Deficient	Suppressed
Putrid	Misleading
Vegetation	Tumultuous
Insurance	Wanton
Portentous	Excruciating

Chapter Thirteen: The Bottoms

Captain Brodst called the company to a halt. The low road that lead down into the murky lowlands, aptly dubbed the Bottoms by both those few who dwelled there and by those who frequented these southerly lands, lay before them.

He cast a glance heavenward, the sun was well past its zenith and the storm clouds of morning were gone. His customary frown lengthened. He reconsidered his alternatives, to take the king's road or to skirt the mire. He had discussed these choices with Keeper Martin, Father Jacob and the other captains the day prior. The obvious choice was to take the short cut through the swamp. They were already behind schedule, yet something Duke Ispeth had told him the night before last was bothering him now.

"Not a single messenger—and few travelers—have come north for more than a week," the duke had said, "'tis a strange occurrence indeed."

At the time Captain Brodst hadn't given it much thought, he had been tired and angry. Duke Ispeth could be a stubborn man when he wanted to be. Captain Brodst remembered that just after the duke had said that he'd scratched his head and said, "It's probably nothing. In another week or so, I'll probably find that the roads were washed out again... Damned rainy season approaching, you know."

But there was something in the way the old duke had said it that told Captain Brodst he didn't really believe what he'd just said. It was true Duke Ispeth was eccentric and suspicious of everyone; even so, Captain Brodst had never seen anyone as agitated as he'd seen the duke that night. He had ranted and raved for hours. He had told them about reports of strange travelers passing through his lands at night, peasants complaining that whole crops were disappearing and many other things.

Captain Brodst took in a deep breath. If the weather had been better, surely they would have been ahead of schedule and he could have opted to skirt the swamps. He had discussed this route with King Andrew because they both feared the closeness of the rainy season. He found it ironic that since the rainy season had arrived early, that he now seemed forced to make a completely wrong choice in an attempt to save time.

None of this worrying will save time, he told himself. They were at least one day behind schedule and needed to make up for lost time. The only way to do it would be to turn south. He gave the signal, pointed to the southernmost road, then spurred his mount on. In a few hours he planned to call a halt for the evening and, by mid-morning of the second day along this route, they should enter the outer mires.

***

The passage along the rolling hills that gradually sloped down into the dreaded Bottoms was moderately paced. Unfortunately, the seasonal rains returned with vigorous fury, forcing a deficient, sluggish rate upon the travelers. But fortunately, after several hours of intense storms, high winds carried the storm front away to leave the skies clear and the grounds muddied though passable.

The group escaped from the confines of heavy cloaks, dropping hoods and loosening the ties about the neck as the air grew warm. Adrina had been in a pensive mood all through the morning. Her thoughts were with Emel. She felt so alone without him and what made this even worse was that everyone around her seemed to notice it, especially Keeper Martin and Father Jacob.

Adrina's unease began to grow as they moved ever closer to the Bottoms, and not only because the thought of traveling through such a place filled her mind with dread. She had been counting on the extra days the longer route around the mires would have provided. The road through the Bottoms would only hasten them to Alderan and this more than anything else filled her mind with alarm.

Keeper Martin, who had been keeping a watchful eye on her and not letting her out of his sight, spoke, "There is nothing to fear, dear, the passage through the mires will be swift and we'll be smelling sea breezes before you know it."

Adrina expressed a sour grimace in response. Keeper Martin may have had an intuitive wisdom, but she knew better than to think there was nothing out there. The putrid smell of rotting vegetation that the wind carried had to be hiding something.

Father Jacob added to the keeper's words, his voice trembling with emotion, "He is right Princess Adrina. Tonight we will stay at a palace of such great beauty that it rivals that of Imtal's. And, Baron Fraddylwicke is a most excellent host."

"Imtal is hardly beautiful," said Adrina.

Father Jacob burst into laughter and said cheerfully, "The palace once belonged to King Jarom the First of Vostok before he lost the lands to the Kingdom long, long ago. At one time, it was the gateway into the whole of the South. The Lord and Lady Fraddylwicke await us…"

His voice trailed off, but Adrina thought she had heard him finish with, "or so I do fear."

"And it has only fallen into the mire three times since then," said Captain Brodst, adding melancholy to the cheer.

Surprised at the Captain's joining in, Adrina said nothing.

"A trivial fact, I assure you," said Keeper Martin, "it was rebuilt each time with increasing care and magnificence."

Adrina smiled and responded, "I can't wait to see it. It sounds wonderful." She added for the keeper's benefit, "Full of history."

Her thoughts took a turn toward expectations and away from disappointment and unease. She was again surprised that Captain Brodst had spoken to her.

"His scowl is his shield," Adrina whispered to herself.

Adrina relaxed in her saddle and soaked up some of the warm air. She undid the ties on her cloak and removed it. However, the warmth that had fed their momentary good spirits came to a quick and not-at-all-subtle end. The ground seemed to readily suck up the warmth and a chill rapidly returned.

***

The long file entered the outer mire. The coolness of the air entwined with the warmth of the ground caused wisps of mist to swirl underfoot even in the early hours of afternoon, giving the area an eerie haze. Adrina felt her body begin to shiver uncontrollably at the cool touch, a touch similar to the play of cold fingers along the exposed areas of her skin.

She pulled her cloak tightly about her and brought its hood up stout, retreating far into the recesses of the cowl as she had this morning. Although the cloak was still moist from the rain, it did manage to provide a little bit of extra warmth. She was thankful for its touch of comfort and hopeful that they would reach the castle soon for she was growing very weary. She sank languidly into the leathers of a saturated, irritating saddle, almost wishing that she had heeded Emel's words and her common sense and remained in Imtal.

Torches were mustered from the supplies and spread through the long line as insurance that, should the mists turn to fog, the group would not get lost. Captain Brodst, using his flint and steel and a few pieces of his precious stock of dry kindling—some of the torches had gotten damp—lit the initial torch, which he passed to the sentinel to bear at the front of the column. For the present, this was the only one to be lit. The others were not yet needed.

The sun's rays were soon lost in a shroud of haze and the hours appeared to drag by. Dampness was so thick in the air that moisture sank into the very souls of those present. Adrina was caught up in deep feelings of portentous dread and she petted her mare's mane to soothe it—or so she told herself. But it was really herself that she sought to calm, to rid her mind of the eerie thoughts it held.

She tried to think pleasant thoughts. She didn't like the swamp they traversed and she liked the dense fog even less. The combination of the two elements overwhelmed her mind and only the thought of the castle that lay somewhere ahead in the distance turned her woes toward eventual ease.

She could imagine the Lord and Lady of the castle, him dressed in a purple overcoat and a blue silk shirt, his court best, and her in the long flowing gown of the day, properly coordinated with the purple and blues of the Lord Fraddylwicke, her attendants forever at her side. She imagined their greeting a grand affair at the great palace gates. The castle walls were not a dead and dreary gray but cheerful silver.

They marched further and further into the mire. It seemed as if they had suddenly delved under a great thick blanket of endless gray. Captain Brodst was forced to call another halt. The double file that they had begun the gradual descent into the mire with was dispensed and a long, drawn-out single file unfolded into the shadows.

Torches were ignited from the sentinel's and though this would have been reassuring under most circumstances, it only assisted the uncanny veil's pervasion of their thoughts.

Progress through the ever-thickening sheets of fog materialized as a feeble inching forward. The cries of the cricket and the frog, the buzzing of insects and the stirrings of other smaller beasts stopped. Only the sloshing of the horses' hooves and boots on the soggy trail remained and it was as if nature itself had paused, waiting for the next puff of freshness and life.

Adrina witnessed the line of lights assemble in front of and behind her. Then, as she watched, the former disappeared one by one into the veil ahead. Those behind she didn't turn to look at.

Carefully following the movements of those ahead when it was her turn, she coaxed her mount by gently slapping it with the reins to start it moving at a relaxed gait. Still she stroked the animal's mane with her free hand. Briefly she looked back now to ensure that the rider behind her noted her passage and followed her lead.

She gazed intently ahead and tried to maintain a bearing on the dim glow of the torch Keeper

Martin carried in front of her. The fog seemed to swallow any hint of the flame, leaving only a slight trace of its glow to guide her movements. The pace appeared to quicken instantly to a gallop and then decrease suddenly to a slow trot, making it extremely difficult for her to preserve the integrity of the file. She wondered how the rider behind her faired in her wake. She hoped that the other could sustain a bearing on her torch but for now she dared not look back for fear of losing sight of the elusive glow in front of her.

The cold mire air grew steadily damp and stagnant as the last remaining hints of the earlier wind disappeared for good. Adrina began to shiver uncontrollably once more. It was as if unseen hands groped their way across her skin and the touch was cold and sinewy.

She tried to find warmth and security in her heavy hooded cloak but she found none. Then just when she thought she could tolerate no more, it was as if those same unseen hands had reached out and grasped her throat, squeezing down with slow, firm pressure.

Suddenly she was afraid to move. What if she raised her hands to her neck and really did find an unseen hand gripped about her throat? But what if it was only her imagination? What then? She wanted to scream out for help, to lash out at the unseen specter, to cry out to the dead land that she did not want it to claim her.

She began to whimper and plea with the unseen hands to release her but this only caused a flood of suppressed emotions—three years of pain and anguish, sorrow and denial—to descend upon her. The dead, gray walls of Imtal were around her, looming up dark and deadly before her—like in her dreams—and all the land was dead and she, Adrina, was dead.

The specter was there with her—like in her dreams—to take her away. But now she didn't want the specter to take her away. The prune-faced man with his twisted wooden staff had saved her before, but he wasn't here now and this wasn't a dream. She began to scream. Frantically she kicked her mount and pulled on the reins sharply. Her shrill scream cut short by a rationalization that came too late.

The horse beneath her, confused by the mixture of opposing signs given it, reared upward. To regain a tight grip on the reins, Adrina twisted the leathers in her hands. This again sent misleading signals to the confounded and uneasy animal beneath her. It reared again.

A second pull on the reins caused the mare to shift sideways as it landed. The steed stumbled, and then faltered as it lost its balance on the uneven roadside. Adrina's tumultuous, wanton eyes spun around as horse and rider tumbled.

No longer a participant, Adrina became an observer. The torchlight seemed to dance around in circles before her as she felt herself falling to the ground. Her head was still spinning and her thoughts yet dazed as she landed with a splash into the murky waters and mud of the mire.

In a blur of frenzied thought, she felt herself sinking downward. A split second passed and she relived the fall into the water, eyes wide, cheeks puffed gasping at air, hands flailing, the light of the torch spinning wildly before her and then dying the instant it hit the dark waters with a sizzle.

A scramble to free feet from stirrups ended as she felt the movement of her body come to a sudden stop. Had she hit bottom? Was this it?

She held all the time in the world in the palm of her hands and she released a sigh of thankfulness, cut short by the horse landing on top of her with a horrific crunch. Adrina's pain was sudden, excruciating and vividly real as her world careened to darkness.

Chapter 13: Word Search

Can you find these words in the puzzle?

Customary	Coordinated	Lowlands	Duke
Mire	Sentinel	Fraddylwicke	Castle
Deficient	Suppressed	Mellack	Bottoms
Putrid	Misleading	Messenger	Horses
Vegetation	Tumultuous	Captain Brodst	Baron
Insurance	Wanton	Swamp	Journey
Portentous	Excruciating	Ispeth	Dangerous
Kingdom	Elves	Queen	Portcullis
Xith	Swords	Robert	Stanek

```
D W E T S I L L U C T R O P X Z C Q F E H Y U P L
N B E W A N T O N G Y U S R V C N K L W S H U N C
O A C F O P L M B X Z Q E L O W L A N D S A S N A
R O T P L S E N T I N E L F R U Y X C V D J W O P
A M N X S Y J J K O T U M U L T U O U S E A C B T
B N E H U Y E I S P E T H Z E B R A T P R T H O A
R A I N E G H P Y K J L O P X B R W O A D R E A I
Q P C B M N U A D M E B U F D H O R S E S D A N N
C A I T R T E S E R G H J T Y U T D D E V M G L B
L K F I R O E S T J J O U R N E Y R R B F I N Z R
S L E I K S S R A K E X Z S N E R T P I C R I V O
B K D I S E T O N I L B C T W N Y R E S H E T K D
K J R V N K A B I N V S O T U A B D R U A A A E S
R N G T Y C N E D G E U Q U E S M A N P T R I A T
D F E X Z I E R R D S W O R D S F P T P A B T S E
L R K N E W K T O O Z B F R E A N I P R O C U U V
I A N M W L Q Z O M Q U E E N O L D X E B G R O R
N A N N E Y E K C A L L E M I S S T L S X U C R Z
S B E C E D S R H K E W F T B Y U T I S O P X E X
U H K S G D J O B K L O A R S V S C Y E U K E G J
R F U D E A A N M J U T I E A A S W Q D T R X N U
A N D E W R U N C I E F N B C U S T O M A R Y A L
N Z W Q R F T R G G U K C B W D W A S R J O E D F
C O O R D I M H E E S S M O T T O B T O N Y D O N
E D W A R D E V X I R X I T H G N I D A E L S I M
```

Words to Watch

Cautiously	Reverently	Behemoth
Content	Twinge	Hearth
Arcane	Aspiration	Assortment
Clapboarded	Profound	Generation
Exterior	Periodically	Jaded
Elongated	Impressionable	Grimace
Respective	Coastal	Perish

Chapter Fourteen: Rest's End

A full day had passed before Xith felt strong enough to continue the journey northward, but in the three days since he and Vilmos had made excellent progress. They were now in the land known as South Province, a holding of Great Kingdom. The wounds Xith had suffered at the hands of the Wolmerrelle were healing nicely and now he looked to the days ahead.

The evil presence that had been with them those many days seemed to be gone—gone with Vangar Forest. Xith knew that all too soon the gentle wind-blown plains of this section of South Province would be gone as well. Their journey was taking them north to Great Kingdom and west to the great sea.

Soon it would be time to again work on awakening the power within the boy. Xith knew he must do this slowly and cautiously. To prepare Vilmos for the task ahead, one that only he could do, Xith must make the boy face his fears. In the end, there would be nowhere left to run *from*, only places to run *to*.

***

Vilmos had never been beyond the limits of the secret place he traveled to in his dreams, the confines of which he had been content to live in and *would* have been content to live in for the rest of his life. Suddenly a new world was opening to him. In it, he discovered new definitions of the boundaries around him and a thirst for knowledge of the outside world. The great windswept plains of South Province were truly beautiful—and a far stretch from the lands of desolation described in the Great Book.

Vilmos listened intently to the shaman's words. Concentrating on this gave him something to focus on, which made it easier to forget all that was behind him.

"The element of fire is the easiest of the arcane elements to grasp initially. It is also the trickiest to control because of the tremendous raw power it taps," Xith had warned him and Vilmos had taken this to heart. After only his third attempt at producing a spark to ignite wood he had performed, "well" as the shaman had put it, "magnificently" as he put it.

He had mastered his first incantation—the first incantation of the element fire. He could now touch delicate power to wood with apparent ease and produce a soft red-orange blaze. Vilmos looked forward to the next lesson, which Xith promised he would teach him soon.

Now it was time for a reprieve from the heavy cares of the world. Before they moved on to the next lesson, Xith had told Vilmos he intended to take them to a place where they could rest for a time.

Ahead in the distance lay a rustic trade center. It was built along the eastern bank of a river, near a ford. Its three small buildings in various stages of decay stood at the fore of the road, huddled around a two-story clapboarded building on which hung a tiny sign that read simply 'Inn, All Welcome.' Other than this sign the settlement was void of all appearances of habitation.

Closer inspection of the small inn showed that, although it was in an equal state of disrepair as the buildings surrounding it, it was a relatively new structure. Xith paused momentarily in the middle of the path and turned to look at Vilmos, then raised the hood of his cloak up over his head and pulled it forward to hide his face in the shadows it created. He motioned for Vilmos to do likewise. The sense of caution in Xith's features told Vilmos to act without hesitation.

The interior of the inn was as untidy and unsightly as the exterior. The ground floor was largely dominated by an open, dimly lit chamber that contained several tables and many chairs, which were twisted and broken. Near an elongated staircase that led to the second floor sat a portly man upon a lonely unbroken chair. In front of him was the sole upright table.

The obese man, who Vilmos surmised to be the inn keep, had a rather unpleasant odor about him. He didn't budge until he heard the sound of coinage dropping onto his tabletop and even then his only action was to point to the stairs, then raise three of his chubby fingers to indicate the respective room number.

Without a word, the weary travelers climbed the stairs and went to room number three. They closed and bolted the door behind them. Though it was only midday they found sleep came very easily, and it was not until many hours later that either stirred.

Vilmos awoke to find Xith staring at him.

"No dreams," Vilmos whispered reverently, as he had each day upon awaking since joining Xith. Then he turned frank eyes to Xith. "Where are we?"

"We have reached the edge of the disputed lands."

"The Borderlands," exclaimed Vilmos. "Bandit Kings and Hunter Clan!"

"No, not the Borderlands of the North, but—"

Vilmos cut Xith short, "—Then the stories are true?"

"Vastly overstated."

"Well, are the stories I heard true or not?... Tales of great heroes of the Borderlands wielding giant battle swords and fighting evil two-headed..." Vilmos didn't finish the sentence.

"Those times are no more," said Xith, a twinge of sadness or perhaps longing in his voice—Vilmos could not tell which. "We are nearing the disputed lands of the South. Here only brigands and a few traders remain. But we are only going to skirt the edge of this area. It is the fastest way to the sea."

Vilmos had never seen the sea, and in his wildest aspirations he had never thought he would. "The sea, really the sea?"

"We are at a last stopping place before we enter what was once the Alder's Kingdom, but is now mostly ruins, except for Alderan."

"Tell me more, please." Vilmos was babbling excitedly.

"There isn't all that much to tell. Besides, your version of the truth would vary greatly from mine. You will see soon enough. We must turn our attention to other things first though," Xith said, a far off look in his eyes. "*Are you there?*" he called out in a scarcely audible voice.

"What do you mean?" asked Vilmos, responding not to the question but to the previous statement.

"Nothing. Rest," said Xith, relief in his voice, "we have a long trip ahead of us in the morning."

Vilmos sensed something was wrong, but whatever it was it seemed out of his grasp. He leaned back, touched head to pillow and closed his tired eyes once again. Images of the day's adventure danced before his sealed lids—the most profound of which was the image of the burly looking innkeeper whose figure played ominously in his thoughts, with his fat hands raised, pointing at him, provoking him, warning him.

After what seemed hours of restless tossing and turning, Vilmos opened his eyes in frustration and sat up in bed. The last light of day still had not given way to the darkness of night and as Vilmos peered about the room, he was shocked to find himself alone. Xith was gone.

Vilmos was puzzled. Would Xith leave him? Maybe he went to relieve himself or something, Vilmos thought. He ran into the hall, but found only greetings of darkness.

"Xith," called out Vilmos in a weak, half-whispered hiss, "Xi-ii-tttthhh."

Frustrated he sat back on the bed, curled his feet up tight and wrapped his hands around his legs. He sat this way for hours, watching the sun slowly disappear behind the neighboring building. Periodically he looked toward the closed door.

The shadows in the room began to take on an eerie perspective, casting odd thoughts into his impressionable young mind. A half-burnt stub of a candle lay atop the stand beside the bed. Vilmos reached out and grabbed it. He thrust it back into the pricket it had been removed from, with the apparent intent of replacing it though the new one had never been brought and the old one had never been discarded. With a flick of absent thought, Vilmos sparked it to life.

The brilliant orange of the flame danced in front of his eyes as if it played out a song to him. Vilmos was captivated and motivated by it. Yet a heavy breath unknowingly extinguished its fragile flame, forcing him to re-ignite it. It had been quite accidental, but Vilmos was amused by it. He took to blowing the candle out and then lighting it again and again with his mind. He laughed a soft, silent chuckle to himself as he did this.

He played with the candle for a time, flicking it off and on, the light of the fire reflecting off his face in the otherwise dark chamber.

Mesmerized by the candlelight, following its on and off blink, eventually, quite accidentally and without even realizing it, Vilmos learned to gingerly manipulate the flame with his mind. He could put it out and then touch it again with his power to relight it, which was quite an accomplishment if only he would have realized it.

With a sudden twist the doorknob turned and the door opened. Vilmos heard voices from the hall.

"I'm sorry I couldn't be of much help old friend. I'm sure you are right. Alderan is the key. They'll surely travel along the coastal highway."

"Goodnight Misha. I am glad your other guests decided to depart ahead of schedule," Xith said. He laughed as he slipped into the room, and then took a sip of the drink in his cupped hand. "We will have to do this again sometime.

"And goodnight to you to. Thank you. You have again done well. I truly did not expect to see you so soon. Guard well the final two scrolls. I will not see you again until after the Autumnal Equinox—after all this is behind us." Xith whispered the last in a voice barely audible, and then took another swig from the half-empty mug he cradled almost tenderly. He waved and then closed the door, trying only now to be quiet.

The scene was quite comical when Xith turned around and prepared to creep to his bed. Vilmos was waiting, and Xith could only smile as a child caught in the act of doing something he knows he's not supposed to be doing. Without a word Xith crossed to the bed opposite Vilmos, sat upon it, blew out the candle Vilmos held and then lay back and closed his eyes.

***

Xith opened the door and pointed down the hall. A heavy sweet aroma filled the air in the hallway and Vilmos' stomach began to growl as he inhaled the first mouth-watering breath. However, before Vilmos could think of food, he had to attend to more immediate matters.

He returned a short while later with a smile on his face and a hand on his belly, a sign that he was hungry. Xith lead him down the stairs to the kitchen from which the aroma rose. The behemoth of a man Vilmos had seen upon their arrival and knew only as the innkeeper was busily working over a brightly burning hearth. Only today, he did not seem so unfriendly and detached as he had the previous evening.

Vilmos scrutinized the small kitchen. He could have sworn he had heard more than two voices last night.

"Beautiful morning Mish'!" Xith exclaimed. He walked over to the large man and patted him on the back.

The innkeeper, Misha, smiled and tossed Vilmos a wink, then he showed the two to a table that was tucked cleanly away in one of the kitchen's many nooks. While they ate, Misha stuffed several satchels with fresh baked breads, smoked meats and an assortment of various other foodstuffs. The aromas wafted through the air to the place where Vilmos and Xith sat and mingled with the pleasant smells already present, creating a feast for the senses of a king. And they both ate like one.

Not long after breakfast, Xith and Vilmos departed the inn. Misha had graciously offered them his wagon, and although old, worn and led by a pair of jades, the wagon was comfortable, and riding proved a very great respite from walking.

Vilmos thought Xith had been rather rude for not introducing him to his apparently good friend. He tossed Xith a snarled grimace but then turned to other subjects, visions of what lay ahead. Although he had never been to the Alder's Kingdom, he knew much about its lore from the Great Book. The Alder had been a very wise king. In signing the treaty with the southern kingdoms, he had ended the longest and bloodiest war in the history of all the lands.

The Race Wars, as they were later called by those few who had survived, had lasted generations. During that time, whole peoples and nations had perished.

A nearly forgotten lesson echoed in Vilmos' mind. He thought of the once great kingdoms of the North. Lycya mightiest of the kingdoms swallowed by barren desert. Queen of Elves and all her people washed into West Deep. North Reach and the clans over-mountain consumed by the twenty-year snow. And, he thought about the Alder.

Xith drove the pair of jades faster than they seemed to want to go. Vilmos knew without doubt the rest was over. Something dread lay ahead, but what it was he did not know.

Chapters 13 and 14: Review Questions

1. What does the author mean when he says Captain Brodst has a customary frown?

2. Why does Adrina feel uneasy when she rides through the rolling hills toward the Bottoms?

3. What do you think caused Adrina to feel unseen hands grabbing for her? Have you ever felt like that?

4. What happens to Adrina when she lets her fears take over?

5. Why does Xith feel he must make Vilmos face his fears?

6. The Great Book of Sever describes the lands to the north as a place of desolation. Why do you think it's important that Vilmos learn the truth about the outside lands?

7. When Vilmos sees the innkeeper, what does he assume and later learn?

8. When Vilmos recalls what the Great Book says about the Alder Kingdom and the Race Wars, what do you think is the point of the lesson that he remembers?

Words to Watch

Disaster	Overcast	Devastating
Despair	Frazzled	Treachery
Turbulent	Haggard	Infection
Desperate	Debris	Concentrated
Fatigue	Invaluable	Huddled
Exhaustion	Waned	
Anguish	Horizon	

Chapter Fifteen: Disaster

Water, dark and icy cold, surrounded Seth. He groped for the surface, his lungs hot and ready to explode. His head stung, his vision clouded. Pain and darkness sought to overcome him. Then just when he thought his lungs would explode, he broke the surface and gasped for air.

Despair filled his mind as turbulent waters pulled him under again. Wildly, he grabbed at the surface, both arms flailing frantically. His hand found something wet and rough. He latched onto it. Coughing and choking, he held on.

The night above the water, nearly as dark as the world beneath the water, offered him little relief. Seth cursed his foolhardiness. He hadn't expected an ambush so soon after departing Kapital and somehow Seth knew he should have. He remembered little of how he had come to be in the water. One minute he had been standing on the deck of the Lady L, Sailmaster Cagan at his side, preparing to make one last desperate stand. The next, a sharp sudden pain in his legs and then the long plunge into cold deep water.

Seth suddenly realized had no idea if anyone else had survived. He lashed out with his mind, *Sailmaster Cagan? Galan?*

Seth felt something pass underneath him, and then touch his legs. Fatigue, disorientation and panic overwhelmed him. Sailmaster Cagan had told him about dark beasts beneath the waters. Creatures called krens that fed on all manner of beast alike. His left arm had caught a blade and his leg—*his right leg*—was gouged from thigh to calf.

Unwisely, Seth kicked out with his feet and slapped the water with his free hand. He lost his grip and again slipped beneath the dark waters. He reached for the surface and the handhold. The piece of wreckage had to be there; it just had to be.

Seth broke the surface, only for an instant, only long enough to fill his lungs with air and calm the red-hot fire in his chest. Then storm-tossed seas pulled him under again.

Great-Father, I cannot fail. My need is great! he called out in despair.

Seth? called out a voice weak in his mind. *Seth?*

His thoughts spun. He reached out, a hand found his.

Bryan?

Yes. Kick harder, I'll need your help. I can't do this alone. Grab on, hold on, don't let go... Just a little more... Just a little more... Seth, you must help me.

With Bryan's help, Seth crawled onto the small section of wreckage. He lay on his back, panting, for many long minutes. Exhaustion nearly carried him away to sleep, but he fought to maintain consciousness. *Did anyone else survive?*

I'm not sure, I saw you get knocked into the sea as the mast crumbled, and I panicked. Everything after that is a blur. The ships are all gone. Fire and water took them.

What about Sailmaster Cagan?

Seth, I don't know... It seems he went down with the Lady L, said Bryan. He paused, his mind filled with obvious anguish. *How did they know we had begun the journey? There were so many, so many…*

Seth found sudden resolve. *We survived Bryan. We have not failed yet… Wait. Did you feel that? The anguish, the sadness.*

That's me, Seth. I'm sorry, I'll shield my thoughts if…

No, someone is out there… Seth turned his thoughts inward and sought to concentrate his will. Then he groped outward with his mind, straining to maintain his strength while he searched. *Galan? Yes—yes, it is… By the Father, she lives!*

Seth pressed his weight against tired arms and sat. He stared into the inky darkness of a largely overcast night sky. He saw little, his mind filled in the pieces. *Wait, someone else is with her… She's holding Everrelle afloat… Galan won't last much longer. She's exhausted.*

Frantically, Bryan and Seth paddled with their hands through choppy waters. It seemed with waves slapping against the makeshift raft, they barely moved at all. Then suddenly two dark shapes appeared out of the gloom. Everrelle, barely conscious, was near death and brave Galan was utterly exhausted from the struggle to keep two afloat in turbulent waters.

***

The night passed with eerie swiftness. Seth awoke to find a midday sun. Images from the previous day seemed a crazed blur, but the ache of his body told him it had all been real. For an instant, Seth felt sure he was alone, and then he saw the others. They were the last survivors. Frazzled and haggard from battle and exposure to the sea only four lingered in life, only these four that had escaped. Now, faith in their service would take them to safety or deliver them from life.

Still exhausted, Bryan and Galan slept. Everrelle, weak from blood loss, slipped in and out of delirium. Seth turned bleary eyes to the sun, its warmth on his face felt good. He remembered now that during the night he had prayed for the day to end the bitter cold. He removed his cloak, which was still mostly wet, and allowed the sun to chase away any remnants of the night's chill. Then he worked to bind wounds that were already festering.

Each of his companions had many injuries—bruises, scrapes, lacerations—which proved to him how desperate the battle had really been and how miraculous it was that anyone still lived. Everrelle was by far in the worst condition. Her right hand was missing four fingers. Seth was sure she must have reached out to block a blow and instead met the steel of a blade. Using strips of cloth from his robe, he did the best he could to wrap her hand. He hoped it would help stay the infection. He turned to Galan next, Bryan afterward. His own wounds he bound last.

Scattered debris from the great ships that the dark deep waters had claimed during the night was all around them. Seth worked against fate to gather what he could. As he worked, he thought of Cagan standing defiantly at the helm of the Lady L. He told himself that was how he wanted to remember the kind sailmaster and all the others that had perished with him. In the end, his search turned up an invaluable prize, a water bag. Half full, but still a water bag. He put it beside the one Bryan had managed to escape the Lady L with, and thanked Great-Father for his good fortune.

The day grew long. The utter exhaustion that held the others found Seth. Unwillingly, he slipped into delirium.

Days passed. Everrelle's condition worsened. Seth, Galan and Bryan took turns at the healing art, but, weak from battle and hunger, they could offer little. Unbelievably, the raft held together with little more than prayers had kept them afloat through those endless days.

Seth had held the hope that land was just over the next crest of the rolling waves or just beyond the next horizon. Bryan and Galan had also been hopeful. But days of nothing save dark waters had tainted that hope and the possibility of safe landfall waned. Now Seth could only lie idle with all his energy drained. Only his training kept his mind semi-clear and his thoughts open. *I am Brother Seth of the Red, First of that order, Queen's Protector*, he repeated many times in his mind.

He sought to cleanse his mind of questions he didn't want to answer. Nonetheless, the questions came. The ambush set by King Mark at the hand of Sathar the Dark had been too well planned. How could the enemy have known their plans so precisely? Was there a traitor among them? Had there been a traitor on the Lady L leading the enemy to them?

No, it can't be, it just can't be. The thought of a traitor having been among them was too painful for Seth to consider. Brother did not betray brother. *No, I must focus.* Seth returned to the cleansing meditation.

Seth, came the whisper into his mind.

I am Brother Seth of the Red, First of that order, Queen's Protector. I must maintain clear thoughts...

SETH?

Yes, my brother I am still here.

Seth, what will it be like in this land of Men? asked Galan.

Still lost in his meditation, it took Seth a moment to slip back into reality, a task accomplished only after Galan repeated her question. Seth said, *It will be different, far different from anything we have ever seen that is for sure. Long ago our people often journeyed to their villages and cities. Our lands and cultures were close together then. It had been a peaceful time, but then came the Great Wars. The last and most devastating treacheries were the Race Wars during which Man drove all their distant cousins away. Into the far corners of the world we fled and never in over five hundred years have we ventured back into their lands.*

Seth felt Galan fight to remain coherent. Galan asked, *What did you learn during those many weeks you studied them? Do you really think they will help us? Or will it all be for nothing...*

Her faith was waning and Seth knew this. *Once we explain what is taking place, it will be their cause as it is ours. They must aid us. But it could take a long time to explain. These Men,*—Seth said the word with distaste—*prefer to stay out of the affairs of others until they are sure they have a marked interest in what is taking place. They often wait until it is too late.*

Seth, began Galan, there was a serious note in the unspoken voice, "*there is something I should tell you that I haven't, something I overheard*—

—*I do not wish to know thoughts that I was not meant to. Some things are best left unknown.*

Like why you prepared for a journey to the lands of Man even before Queen Mother consulted High Council. And why your lessons began even before we learned of Sathar's return.

Seth was unsure whether he should voice the truth or not—*but what did it really matter anyway?*

There is much more in peril than our homes and lands. Queen Mother knew this.

Seth, I grow tired. I must rest. Will you play the image Brother Liyan gave to you, the image of the green forest? I wish to dream...

***

Seth looked to Galan, who was still sleeping, and wondered if dreams of the forest still swept through her mind. He knew little of the sea and winds, but, unlike Bryan and Galan, he had been on the canals of Kapital with Sailmaster Cagan. He used a makeshift hook and tied bits of colored cloth to it, then cast out his line, a length of string from his robe. Over these past days, he had enjoyed no luck and while it truly seemed there was no life in the deep sea, he was not about to give up.

A hazy dawn eventually gave way to day as the sun made its inevitable climb. With irony, Seth remembered now that he had once prayed for the day's arrival to end the bitter cold of night. But the night didn't steal precious moisture from his weary body, the sun did.

The day gradually grew hot and dry. Seth found that his thoughts were beginning to wander. He maintained consciousness, but only barely so while he cast the line out and pulled it in slowly, as he had once been shown.

At one point, out of the corner of his eye, Seth saw Bryan moving about the raft, but inevitably as the sun beat down upon him, thirst and hunger took over. His thoughts began to wander and shift despite his best efforts. Seth attempted to clear his thoughts, but this required a complete conscious effort, which, under the torment of the blistering sun, with strength draining from his body little by little, Seth could not give it. He could only mourn the loss he could do nothing to regain. He perceived himself as a hapless child. He, First of the Red, with all his knowledge and skills could not resolve their dilemma.

Seth soon found himself drifting back to sleep.

We're in danger, warned Bryan. *Krens!*

Seth came alert in an instant. It seemed he had just closed his eyes, but then he took note of the light of a virgining day on the horizon. Then suddenly Bryan's warning registered in his mind. *By the Father! Galan, Everrelle!... Everrelle?*

Galan awoke. Everrelle didn't. For some reason one of the great gray beasts began attacking the bottom of the raft. Bryan pulled in the fishing line. Seth noticed there was something on it. Seth asked, *You caught something?*

Bryan started to reply, *In a way—*

Bryan's voice was drowned out by Galan's scream. *Dear Father. Everrelle, Everrelle?*

Galan directed thoughts to Seth. *The infection it's worse...* Then she turned back to Everrelle. *Stay with me, stay with us, don't go. 'We'll survive the journey together,' you said. Hold on, promise me you'll hold on...*

Another of the gray beasts that lurked just beneath the surface of the water nudged the raft.

Get Everrelle away from the edge! exclaimed Bryan.

Days without food meant exhaustion. Galan too was exhausted, and the exhaustion only magnified her alarm and her panic. Seth could see it in her eyes. He directed Bryan to crawl to the other side of the raft and help Galan with Everrelle. Then he concentrated on angry thoughts and sent them into the minds of the dark shapes beneath the water.

The raft shook as it was buffeted by tail and fin. Angrily and relentlessly, Seth, Galan and Bryan beat at the dark shapes until the raft shook no more. The three stood quietly, huddled together, and stared into the dark waters.

One by one, fatigue overwhelmed them. Bryan was the first to collapse, Seth the last. Silence followed.

Galan broke the long silence, with a very soft whisper, *Everrelle is gone... She promised she'd hold on, she promised.*

Seth didn't answer immediately. Sleep was trying to lull him. He felt Everrelle's passing, but could do nothing more than wish her a safe journey. After a few minutes, he directed a response to Galan, *Sleep, my brother, save your strength.*

Chapter 15: Word Sort

Can you rewrite the word list in alphabetical order? Hint: A to Z.

Disaster
Despair
Turbulent
Desperate
Fatigue
Exhaustion
Anguish

Can you rewrite the word list in alphabetical order? Hint: A to Z.

Overcast
Frazzled
Haggard
Debris
Invaluable
Waned
Horizon

Can you rewrite the word list in reverse alphabetical order? Hint: Z to A.

Devastating
Treachery
Infection
Concentrated
Huddled
Haphazardly
Attention

Can you rewrite the word list in reverse alphabetical order? Hint: Z to A.

Litany
Rhythmic
Uniform
Miracle
Reassuring
Instinctively

Words to Watch

Haphazardly	Litany
Attention	Rhythmic
Uniform	Noticeable
Miracle	Convulse
Reassuring	Comfortable
Instinctively	Unsettling

Chapter Sixteen: Return

"Father Jacob, will she be all right?" demanded Captain Brodst. His heart pounded rapidly in his ears, a lump swelled in his throat. He paced back and forth, and waved a torch haphazardly about in the air, paying little attention to the water and muck that dripped from his uniform. The young Princess Adrina, her face deathlike, was his only concern.

He feared the worst for Adrina as her face grew ashen. He was positive King Andrew would have his head for this. His despair grew, so did his anger and frustration. Again, he yelled at Father Jacob who apparently was not listening to him. "Father, will she be all right?"

Father Jacob had worked frantically ever since Captain Brodst had rescued Adrina from the murky waters of the mire. Although a male, he knew the art of healing well and had attempted to work its miracles on her almost immediately. Yet he was growing annoyed by the captain's repeated inquiries and this distracted him.

"Perhaps, perhaps," he hissed back at the captain, "if you give me some silence!"

Keeper Martin touched a hand to the captain's shoulder and said, "Do not worry so. Father Jacob knows what he is doing. Give him some room and the silence he asks for, then trust in him and Great-Father." Then he returned the captain's cloak and sword belt.

Captain Brodst took the belt and cloak and donned them. He chased off the reassuring hand. He didn't want to be soothed. He wanted Adrina to regain consciousness and to ensure this, he whispered numerous pleas to Great-Father.

There was doubt in Father Jacob's mind as he continued to labor over Adrina, his healing abilities were not as great as those who were of the Mother. Jacob would have offered his soul to have a priestess of the Mother stumble across their path if he hadn't believed that somehow he could save Adrina—after all, she had been in the presage. All he had to do was to overcome his doubt.

Instinctively, Father Jacob had laid Adrina on her side and managed to clear some of the water from her lungs, still she had not regained consciousness, nor did she breathe. Father Jacob could not touch enough of the Mother's will to draw upon her powers to cure. Only after special prayers were sent to Great-Father to give him the extra strength necessary did Jacob begin to chant the incantation—the ancient litany of life and healing. He wouldn't think it odd that fate had brought him to this path until sometime later as he reflected upon this happening.

Erase doubt, he reminded himself, think only of healing and life. He continued the rhythmic chanting.

A noticeable shift swept across Adrina's features, her chest rose once and then fell as her body convulsed. Soon Father Jacob heard the strangled sounds of the girl choking on water still in her lungs. He slapped her back repeatedly and forced her to cough.

Adrina choked on the water she spit up, and gasped frantically for air. She inhaled deeply and rapidly. Violently she vomited the mixture of water and mud she had swallowed—Jacob never broke the rhythmic tone of the litany of life and healing. After a moment, Adrina stopped her convulsing and regained her senses. Tears rolled down her cheeks as she reached up to embrace Father Jacob.

"I'm sorry," she whimpered, "I'm sorry." She closed her eyes briefly against the tears and let the elder hold her.

"Blankets! Get me some blankets, now!" said Father Jacob. He was clearly drained of all his strength. His face was pale and wet with perspiration. He sighed, he had done it, he had succeeded. "We must keep her warm. She will need to get some deep rest soon, and in a warm, comfortable bed."

Silence prevailed for a time afterward as Jacob's words settled on those listening—they must get through this damnable mire and reach the elusive castle somewhere in the distance. Night had settled upon them somewhere during the journey through the mire or perhaps in the frantic moments following Adrina's near fatal accident. Only Father Jacob truly knew how close Adrina had come to death's door, for he was of Great-Father and Great-Father knew all, especially in matters of death.

With unsettling certainty, Father Jacob knew that an unseen evil had been at hand. Great-Father had sensed it and so had he.

The story continues with:

The Kingdoms & The Elves of the Reaches II
Keeper Martin's Tales Book 2

Chapters 15 and 16: Review Questions

1. What happened to Seth and his companions, and who survived the initial disaster?

2. What does Seth do to help ensure the safety of his friends? What would you have done if you were him?

3. Chapter 16 is titled "Return." What event does that hint at?

4. Why didn't Father Jacob perform mouth-to-mouth resuscitation on Adrina when she was pulled from the water?

5. What do you think will happen next to Seth, Adrina, Vilmos, and their friends?

About the Author

Robert Stanek is the author of many previously published books, including several bestsellers. Currently, he lives in the Pacific Northwest with his wife and children. Robert is proud to have served in the Persian Gulf War as a combat crewmember on an electronic warfare aircraft. During the war, he flew numerous combat and combat support missions, logging over two hundred combat flight hours.

His distinguished accomplishments during the Persian Gulf War earned him nine medals, including the United States of America's highest flying honor, the Air Force Distinguished Flying Cross. His career total was 17 medals in only 11 years of military service, making him one of the most highly decorated veterans of the Persian Gulf War.

Overwhelmingly, readers agree that Robert's books are among the best they've ever read. His books have very vocal supporters who aren't afraid to voice their opinion, and they frequently do so in online communities and lists, such as at Amazon.com, where you'll find that his books are consistently listed at the top of their class. Strong reader support has led to strong sales. The worldwide in print total for his books is quickly approaching 2 million.

About Reagent Press

Reagent Press is a small press that publishes both fiction and non-fiction titles. Current fiction titles include *Keeper Martin's Tale* and *Elf Queen's Quest* from the Ruin Mist Chronicles, *The Kingdoms & The Elves of the Reaches Book I* and *Book II* from Keeper Martin's Tales, and *The Elf Queen & The King Book I* and *Book II* from Ruin Mist Tales. Current non-fiction titles include: *Effective Writing for Business, College & Life*, *Essential Windows 2000 Commands Reference*, and *Essential Windows XP Commands Reference*.

Thank you for your continued support! Without the help of you, the reader, we will not be able to produce future works. If you liked this book, please tell your friends!

Ruin Mist Heroes, Legends & Beyond

Just about everyone that has read about Ruin Mist has wondered about the back story, where it all began, how the story all fits together, and now you can find answers in *Ruin Mist Heroes, Legends & Beyond*, a companion volume to the top-selling Ruin Mist books. *Ruin Mist Heroes, Legends & Beyond* allows you to learn about the dark elves of Under-Earth, common trades in the kingdoms, and beasts that go bump in the night. You can read the complete rules for King's Mate: the game, explore dozens of maps detailing the known realms, learn about the author, and more. In short, this is one book you shouldn't be without.

Keeper Martin's Tales

The Kingdoms & the Elves of the Reaches

Inside you'll discover the breathtaking world of Ruin Mist where the mystical and the magical abound, and you'll fall in love with a boy who would become a mage, a princess who is just now seeing the world around her, a warrior elf who undertakes an epic journey, and their friends.

The Kingdoms & the Elves of the Reaches 2

Adrina, Emel, Vilmos, Galan and Seth must survive the greatest challenge Great Kingdom has faced in hundreds of years: the dissolution of the Kingdom Alliance and the battle to save Quashan'. Survival in a changing world depends on their ability to adapt and if they fail, their world and everything they believe in will perish.

The Kingdoms & the Elves of the Reaches 3

Adrina, Emel, Vilmos, Galan and Seth face even greater challenges as their world is transformed. Vilmos, in his quest to become the first human magus in a thousand years, must control the darkness within him. Adrina must accept her place and work together with Emel to help the elves make their plea to Great Kingdom's council. What happens along the way will amaze you.

Ruin Mist Tales

The Elf Queen & the King

The first book on the dark path through the history of Ruin Mist. The Ruin Mist Chronicles begin when the Elf Queen sends the warrior elf, Seth, on a journey to the kingdoms. Legend says that the elves and men have been enemies since the dawn of time, and there are few who remember the time before the Great War that divided the peoples of Ruin Mist.

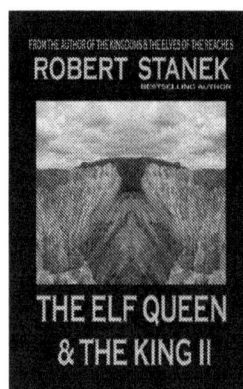

The Elf Queen & the King 2

The mysterious Xith returned from under-mountain just as he said he would. He brought dark news in a dark time, confirming Princess Adrina's worst fears. Something terrible was happening; what it was they were only beginning to understand. Now Adrina, Emel, Xith, Vilmos, and the others must determine the true fate of Alderan as they set out to save Great Kingdom.

Magic Lands

Following the village elder's advice, Ray leaves his home village, setting out for the place lost and deep where he will find a companion for his journey to the stone land and where he will discover that there is no easy path from childhood to manhood. "Beware lashing tail and gnashing teeth," the village elder warns him, "and if Old Bull doesn't get you, Mother Slither surely will."

Win Free Books For Your School!

Help your school win free books! Here's how:

> Create a school Web page featuring Robert Stanek's books and use it to share your experiences reading the books with other students. Send information about your Web page to the address below. Don't forget to mention the Web address— you know that funny line of text that begins with *http://*.

> Write a letter detailing your experiences reading *The Kingdoms & the Elves of the Reaches*. Share your thoughts. Tell us what you liked most about the books. Talk about your favorite characters, events or other elements from the books. Send the letter to the address below.

When you write be sure to tell us the name and address of your school as well as the name of your principal and teacher. Also let us know your first name and grade, but you don't need to put your last name. Here's an example:

> Name/Grade: Mary 4th Grade
> Teacher: Mrs. Brown
> Principal: Mr. Johnson
> School: Silver Creek Elementary School
>   555 Main St., Silver Creek, PA 03557

Send your letter to:

> Reagent Press
> Attn: Books for Schools
> P.O. Box 362
> East Olympia, WA 98540-0362

Good luck! We truly hope your school wins some great free books... Just for entering, you could win a cool Ruin Mist T-Shirt, Hat or Poster from the Ruin Mist Gear Shop (http://www.cafeshops.com/ruinmistgear).

Void where prohibited or restricted by law. Odds of winning approximately 1 in 12. Write to Reagent Press for more details.